President OBAMA

And a New Birth of Freedom

OBAMA'S AND LINCOLN'S
INAUGURAL ADDRESSES
AND MUCH MORE

Joseph Cummins

Collins
An Imprint of HarperCollinsPublishers

For my daughter, Carson

Collins is an imprint of HarperCollins Publishers.

President Obama and a New Birth of Freedom: Obama's and Lincoln's Inaugural Addresses and Much More

Library of Congress Cataloging-in-Publication Data is available.
ISBN 978-0-06-184787-5

1 2 3 4 5 6 7 8 9 10

❖

First Edition

"We here highly resolve that these dead shall not have died in vain; that this nation, under God, shall have a new birth of freedom; and that government of the people, by the people, for the people, shall not perish from the earth."

Abraham Lincoln
Gettysburg Address
November 19, 1863

Contents

January 20, 2009: President Obama is sworn in while his wife, Michelle, holds the Bible from Lincoln's first inauguration and daughters, Malia and Sasha, stand by her side.

1.

Inaugurations, Past and Present

"I do solemnly swear (or affirm) that I will faithfully execute the office of President of the United States, and will to the best of my ability, preserve, protect and defend the Constitution of the United States."

U.S. Constitution, Article 2, Section 1

When Barack Obama took this oath at noon on January 20, 2009, he became the forty-fourth president of the United States to repeat these exact thirty-five words. The words haven't changed since our first president, George Washington, spoke them in New York City on April 30, 1789. A great deal about presidential inaugurations *has* changed over the course of two centuries—their date, where they are held, the ceremonies surrounding them, and the number of people who are able to see and hear them, just for starters. This oath of office, however, as written into the U.S. Constitution, has not changed at all.

Think of the often-violent changes of power that go on routinely in other countries. In many cases, power-hungry factions ignore the will of the people and seize the reins of government by force. Now think of the forty-four U.S. presidents over the course of 220 years, standing in front of the American people, raising their hands, and taking this oath.

As Dr. Donald R. Kennon, chief historian of the United States Capitol Historical Society, says: "Our American Revolution was an experiment to see if the people could govern themselves. And the regular and routine nature of a presidential inauguration reassures the people that the experiment is continuing and succeeding."

"A New Birth of Freedom"

The Joint Congressional Committee on Inaugural Ceremonies (JCCIC) is a committee made up of six senior members of the House of Representatives and Senate. Since 1901, the JCCIC has helped plan inaugural ceremonies surrounding the actual swearing-in of the president. This is because most presidents-elect take their oaths of office at the Capitol Building, the home of the United States Congress.

Since February 2009 marks the two hundredth anniversary of Abraham Lincoln's birth, the JCCIC chose a phrase from Lincoln's Gettysburg Address—"a new birth of freedom"—as the inaugural theme. Lincoln made this famous address during the Civil War. In it, he reminded people that because of the sacrifices of the soldiers who had died in the war helping to free the slaves and preserve the Union, America would experience "a new birth of freedom." Lincoln wanted Americans to remember that the country was founded on the principle of "government of the people, by the people, for the people," and that they shared the responsibility of ensuring that it "shall not perish from the earth."

The JCCIC picked this theme before it was known that Barack Obama would win the 2008 election, but it's fitting for Obama, the first African American president, to have "a new birth of freedom" as an inaugural theme. It is an extraordinary, first-in-our-history occurrence to have an African American president and his family—his wife, Michelle, and his daughters Malia, ten, and Sasha, seven, and their grandmother Marian—in the White House. Barack Obama has talked movingly about how wonderful it will be for his children to live and play freely in a place that was built partly by slave labor.

In fact, slaves and servants were the only African Americans allowed in the White House from its completion in 1800 until the African American writer and abolitionist Frederick Douglass visited in 1865, after Abraham Lincoln's second inauguration. At this time it was the custom of presidents to hold a kind of "open house" at the White House after the ceremonies of inauguration day, allowing the public to greet the newly sworn-in president. That day, Abraham Lincoln was said to have shaken hands with six thousand people. But because he was African American, Frederick Douglass was at first turned away by guards. He was finally able to reach the reception, where Lincoln called him over. Lincoln said to those around him: "Here comes my friend Douglass," and then asked Douglass for his opinion of the speech. "There is no man in the country whose opinion I value more than yours," Lincoln told Douglass. "That was a sacred effort," Douglass replied.

Nevertheless, discrimination continued in the White House, as it did across the land. When President Theodore Roosevelt had dinner with the African American educator, writer, and orator Booker T. Washington in the White House in 1901, one Southern newspaper called it "the most damnable outrage which has ever been perpetrated by any citizen of the United States."

While Obama's election will not end racism, his tenure as president may help Americans come to terms with some of the racial issues that continue to trouble our country.

"I Got Some Game"

As a new United States senator in 2005, Barack Obama wrote in a *Time* magazine essay that he kept a photograph of Lincoln in his office. In the photograph the great president looked very tired, yet he was still smiling. Obama wrote: "On trying days, the portrait . . . soothes me." It made Barack Obama realize that, as Lincoln did, he could "overcome personal loss and remain determined in the face of repeated defeats."

Like Lincoln, Barack Obama got his start in the rough and tumble of Illinois politics and overcame personal hardship in his early life. Also like Lincoln, Obama is known for his speechmaking skills. Obama announced his candidacy for president from the Old State House in the capital of Springfield, Illinois. This was where Lincoln had kept his law offices and worked in the state legislature. Obama was trying to link himself to the beloved sixteenth president of the United States. "In the shadow of the Old State Capitol, where Lincoln once called on a divided house to stand together, where common hopes and common dreams still live," Obama told the crowd, "I stand before you today to announce my candidacy for president of the United States."

There are some experts who say that it is quite daring for Obama to compare his quest to that of the man who many feel is the greatest president in our nation's history. Columbia University historian Eric Foner says that it is "a bit like a basketball player turning up before his first game and saying, 'I'm kind of modeling myself on Michael Jordan.' If you're LeBron James, that works. But people may make the comparison to your disadvantage."

But as Obama said himself, way back in 2004: "I'm LeBron, baby, I can play on this level. I got some game."

Another similarity between Barack Obama and Abraham Lincoln is that they both took over as president during a period when their country was undergoing tumultuous times. By 1860, the Southern states had already begun to leave the Union, setting the scene for the Civil War, which would start barely a month after Lincoln's inauguration. Obama is now president of a country that is fighting two foreign wars and is in the midst of its greatest financial crisis since the Great Depression of the 1930s.

Yet there is one single message exemplified by the actions of both men—a message of unity. "When an election is over," Lincoln once said, "it is altogether fitting for a free people that until the next election they should be one people." On November 4, 2008, when Barack Obama won his historic race for president, he quoted a line from the closing paragraph of Lincoln's first inaugural address. He reached out to both his passionate supporters and those who had not voted for him. "We are not enemies, but friends," he said, and asked his fellow Americans to come together as one.

The historian Doris Kearns Goodwin, in her book *Team of Rivals*, shows how Lincoln picked three political rivals for important positions in his cabinet. Similarly, Obama chose unity over partisan politics by picking his staunch presidential opponent, Hillary Clinton, as his new secretary of state and Republican Ray LaHood as secretary of transportation.

Inaugurations, Past and Present

While the United States Constitution is very specific about the exact words a person needs to say to be sworn in as president, it says little about the ceremonies that should surround the occasion. Therefore, a wide array of rituals and customs has sprung up around presidential inaugurations. The inauguration of President Barack Obama was a celebration—of change, of freedom, and of a new involvement of the people of the United States with their government. To symbolize this, President-elect Obama boarded a train in Philadelphia on the Saturday before his inauguration, stopped in Wilmington, Delaware, to pick up Vice President–elect Joe Biden and his family, then went on to Baltimore, before finally arriving in Washington D.C.

Although two hundred years separate the two events, Barack Obama's journey was made in the same spirit as that of our first president, George Washington, in 1789. Washington—who was even then being called "the father of our country"—was the most beloved and respected man in America. He was the unanimous choice for president among appointed electors. (There was no popular vote at the time.) After the election was held in January 1789, George Washington left his home in Mount Vernon, Virginia, for a two-week trip to New York City, where the first Congress met. Thousands of people lined the road to see him, cheering and tossing flowers and singing. He was rowed across the Hudson River to New York on a barge manned by thirteen sailors, and serenaded by thirteen singing girls. Each represented one of the thirteen states. The girls sang:

Welcome, mighty chief! Once more,
Welcome to this mighty shore!

After that, he went to Federal Hall in downtown New York, stood on a balcony, and was sworn in by Robert Livingston, chancellor of the state of New York. There was no Supreme Court yet, so this was one of the few times when someone other than the chief justice of the United States Supreme Court swore in the president. According to legend, after Washington repeated the thirty-five-word oath, he said: "So help me God." (Most presidents—but not all—have followed their oath by saying this phrase.) Washington then retired to the Senate chambers, where he gave the very first inaugural address in private to the very first Senate and House of Representatives.

In 1800, Congress moved from Philadelphia to the new capital city of Washington, and President Thomas Jefferson became the first president to be sworn in there. Although Washington was sworn in on April 30, Congress passed a law in 1792 making inauguration day officially March 4. This law became part of the Constitution when the Twelfth Amendment was passed in 1804. In those days, when communication and travel were much slower, it was important to have more time between election day and inauguration day. By the twentieth century, with the advent of the automobile, plane, and telephone, it began to seem like four months was too long for a president-elect to wait to take office. In 1933, the Twentieth Amendment was passed to change the date of the inauguration to January 20. If this date falls on a Sunday, the president-elect usually takes the oath of office privately and then has his public swearing-in ceremony on Monday. The next time this will happen is in 2013.

"I Would Much Rather Be in Bed"

There were numerous colorful inaugural balls after Obama's swearing-in. This custom started in the early nineteenth century. The first inaugural ball was held in honor of James Madison's presidency in 1809. The outgoing president, Thomas Jefferson, danced happily, while Madison whispered to a friend, "I would much rather be in bed." Only four hundred people attended that ball, at the price of $4 a ticket. Today, tickets to some balls cost hundreds and sometimes thousands of dollars. For a long time, inaugural balls have been places where people went to see the famous and to be seen themselves. People dress in the height of fashion—or at least try to. In 1861, at a ball following Abraham Lincoln's first inauguration, the *New York Times* complained that "some ladies displayed the bad taste of wearing their rings over their gloves!"

The inauguration of Martin Van Buren in 1837 marked the first time the outgoing and incoming presidents rode together to the Capitol Building for the swearing-in ceremony. This custom has continued to this day. However, presidents are only human. Sometimes the outgoing president doesn't like to spend time with the person who has just beaten him (and who has perhaps said harsh things about him) in a national election. President Herbert Hoover, who hated the policies of the new president-elect, Franklin Roosevelt, refused to speak to Roosevelt on their traditional ride to the Capitol Building in 1933. Hoover just stared straight ahead, and Roosevelt couldn't get him to talk. In the meantime, thousands of people waved at their open limousine and cheered and sang

"Happy Days Are Here Again!" Hoover just kept on sulking. Finally, as Roosevelt later told his secretary, he exclaimed to himself: "Spinach! The two of us simply couldn't sit there on our hands ignoring each other and everyone else. So I began to wave with my top hat."

Ever since Franklin Roosevelt did so in 1933, president-elects and their vice presidents have gone to church services on the morning of their inaugurations. Barack Obama and Joe Biden were no exception. After the service they headed to the Capitol Building. There Vice President Joe Biden was sworn in first, since, if anything happens to the president, the vice president needs to be ready to step in. Then Chief Justice of the Supreme Court John G. Roberts, Jr., administered the oath of office to Barack Obama.

Chief justices have almost always administered the oaths, except on the few occasions when a president has died in office. When President Warren G. Harding died from a heart attack in August 1923, Vice President Calvin Coolidge had a most unusual swearing-in ceremony. He was spending the night at his father's house in a remote Vermont town called Plymouth Notch. The house was so old it had no electricity, no telephone, and no running water. A telegram carrying the news of Harding's death was sent to a town eight miles away and then it finally reached the Coolidge home. Two more urgent telegrams were sent by the attorney general and secretary of state, telling Coolidge he must take the oath of office as soon as possible. One telegram even contained the text of the oath, just in case he needed it. Since Coolidge's father, John Coolidge, was a local justice of the peace, he decided to swear in his son. And so it was that the president was sworn in by his father by the light of a kerosene lamp, at 2:45 in the morning. This is the first and only time a father has ever given the presidential oath of office to his son.

Be Sure to Wear Your Coat and Hat

After Joe Biden and Barack Obama were sworn in, President Obama made his inaugural address to the people, carried live to millions on television and the internet. It's hard to imagine now, but this kind of instant access to history is a big change from how things used to be. In 1925, Americans were able to listen to an inauguration for the first time—Calvin Coolidge's—live on the radio. The first televised inaugural address was that of Harry Truman, in 1948. President Bill Clinton's second inauguration, in 1997, was the first to be streamed live over the internet.

Inaugural speeches have varied greatly. The shortest was George Washington's second address in 1793, only 135 words long. The longest—over eight thousand words and two hours in length—was given by President William Henry Harrison. Unfortunately, Harrison made the speech in freezing cold weather without wearing a hat or a coat, and he died a month later of pneumonia. Ever since then, presidents have kept their speeches relatively short, although weather can play a big role in what happens.

At John F. Kennedy's inauguration in 1961, the sun was shining so brightly into the poet Robert Frost's eyes that he was unable to read "Dedication," the poem he had written especially for the occasion. He instead recited an old poem, "The Gift Outright," from memory. And it was so cold that the army had to use flamethrowers to clear the snow and ice off Pennsylvania Avenue for the inaugural parade. They never did this again because the flames left scorch marks on the pavement!

The inaugural parade has developed over time as well. In the nineteenth century, it occurred before the oath of office was given, as it was the custom for the people to follow the president-elect to the swearing-in site. Now it happens afterward. The custom is for the president and his family to have lunch inside the Capitol Building, as Obama and his family did, and then to have them lead the parade, either walking or riding up Pennsylvania Avenue to the White House.

When the president and his family get to the White House, they stand on a reviewing stand and watch the rest of the parade go by. The parade is usually filled with bands, military formations, elephants or donkeys (to symbolize either the Republican or the Democratic Party), and colorful floats. The inaugural parade has been called "the most history-laden parade in the Western hemisphere, and sometimes one of the most bizarre." The longest parade—four hours and thirty-two minutes—took place at Dwight Eisenhower's 1953 inauguration. Much to the annoyance of the Secret Service, he allowed himself to be lassoed by a cowboy named Monte Montana, something that was definitely not in the script for the day.

All of Us

On inauguration day, perhaps the most impressive sight of all is that of the American people. George Washington's first-ever inauguration in New York City drew only local crowds. Crowds for inaugurations through the early nineteenth century remained relatively low. This is not surprising, given the difficulty of traveling on bad roads with only horses and carriages. But with the coming of the train, car, interstate highway, and airplane, more and more people have flocked to Washington for the inauguration. In the early twentieth century, thousands of people attended. By the 1960s and 1970s, hundreds of thousands were in attendance. Obama's inauguration, which opened up the National Mall to the public for the first time on Inauguration Day, drew over a million proud Americans.

The word *inauguration* comes from a root word in Latin: *augur*. During the times of the ancient Romans, an augur was someone who watched the flights of birds in order to attempt to predict the future. Holding a successful inauguration, then, is a way for us to try to make sure that the signs are favorable for good things to come. When Barack Obama woke up on January 21, he could say with certainty that he'd had the best inauguration that the American people could give him.

Prints & Photographs Division, Library of Congress, LC-USZ62-2006

November 19, 1863: Lincoln delivers his address at the dedication of the Gettysburg National Cemetery.

2.

The Gettysburg Address

"A New Birth of Freedom": Setting the Scene

ABRAHAM LINCOLN gave the Gettysburg Address in the tiny Pennsylvania hamlet of the same name on Thursday, November 19, 1863. While Lincoln gave two elegant and thoughtful inaugural addresses, the Gettysburg Address was a different kind of speech altogether. It was only 272 words long—ten sentences. It took the president only three minutes to deliver it, reading from two pieces of paper that he had pulled from the inside pocket of his jacket. Yet it was not only the greatest speech Lincoln ever gave, but probably the greatest speech made in American history.

On that cool November day in Gettysburg, Abraham Lincoln stood in a graveyard. There he was surrounded by the tombs of seven thousand Union soldiers who had died in the ferocious battle of Gettysburg in July of that year. This battle had stopped the Confederate Army's advance into the North and turned the tide of the Civil War.

The Battle of Gettysburg took place after three years of the most terrible bloodshed the American continent has ever known, with Northern and Southern armies fighting from Pennsylvania to Virginia and from New Orleans to Texas. Abraham Lincoln had experienced some very dark hours when it seemed that the Southern armies and the institution of slavery might prevail. But the victory of General George Meade over General Robert E. Lee changed the course of the war in favor of the Union forces.

After the battle, the Union dead had been carefully identified and then reburied in a new Soldiers' National Cemetery at Gettysburg (now called Gettysburg National Cemetery). Lincoln, along with other famous politicians and speakers, had been invited to dedicate that cemetery.

"Short, Short, Short"

As with many famous historical events, there are numerous legends that have sprung up around the Gettysburg Address. One is that Lincoln scrawled his speech on the back of an envelope as he rode the train down to Gettysburg from Washington D.C. This seems highly unlikely. Lincoln was a careful organizer who understood the power of words better than almost any other U.S. president. He would never have left such an important task to the last moment, especially on a train ride where he would be expected to meet and greet any number of politicians and well-wishers who were also on their way to Gettysburg.

Three or four days before the cemetery dedication, Lincoln told the journalist Noah Brooks that his speech would be "short, short, short" and that it was "written, but not finished." This means that while Lincoln may have put the finishing touches on the speech at the last minute, it was basically written before he even left the capital.

The person who spoke first at the cemetery dedication was not Abraham Lincoln, but the former senator and Harvard University president Edward Everett. His presence has led to another myth about Gettysburg—that Abraham Lincoln was insulted by the organizers of the cemetery dedication because he was not picked as the first speaker. In fact, the cemetery had been paid for by funds raised from the states of those soldiers who had died at Gettysburg. It was not considered an event that would involve the federal government. Lincoln was invited to speak as a courtesy. No offense was intended, and he did not take any.

Edward Everett was a famous speaker who specialized in battlefield topics. He had previously dedicated monuments at such important Revolutionary War sites as Lexington and Concord and Bunker Hill. In an age before television or the movies, people loved to see him because he provided what the historian Garry Wills has called a kind of "docudrama" for his listeners—a sort of reenactment of what happened on the battlefield.

Everett dramatically took his listeners through the events of the three-day battle, step by step. His speech was thirteen thousand words long. He spoke for two hours, and people could not stop listening. He was a tough act to follow. When he sat down, Abraham Lincoln stood. And as he rose to speak, he looked at the graves of the dead soldiers, which were arranged in wide semicircles around a monument to their courage.

"Government of the People"

In the crowd of onlookers—estimated to be fifteen

thousand strong—there were many people who had lost sons, brothers, and husbands at Gettysburg. What could Abraham Lincoln possibly say to these people to help make their grief more bearable?

The average age of a Union or Confederate soldier in the Civil War was eighteen. Many of the soldiers in the graves facing Lincoln were still teenagers when they died. Most of them were from farms or small towns like Gettysburg. They would have had their whole lives ahead of them—except that they had been killed in battle.

Lincoln began his speech by bringing his listeners back—"fourscore and seven years ago," eighty-seven years before—to the time when America was founded. He reminded people that the Declaration of Independence had stated that "all men are created equal," a truly radical idea for the time. However, this idea had not been realized for the African Americans, who were held as slaves, not treated as equals, and denied their rights and humanity. Now "a great civil war" was being fought. The men who inhabited the graves Lincoln could see around him on that November day—as well as the men still fighting the war in battlefields further south—had given "the last full measure of devotion." They had made the ultimate sacrifice by dying for their country. They were the ones who made that ground hallowed (or holy), not Lincoln or Edward Everett or anyone else, no matter how many speeches they made.

All the living could do was work to finish "the great task remaining"—to end the Civil War with a Northern victory. Lincoln looked to the future and vowed that because of the sacrifices of those dead soldiers, America would experience a "new birth of freedom" and discover "that government of the people, by the people, for the people, shall not perish from the earth."

Lincoln finished his speech and sat down.

A surprising myth surrounding Lincoln's Gettysburg Address is that it was not well received. On the contrary, newspaper accounts of the time show that in only three minutes, Lincoln was interrupted five times for applause. Most journalists praised him. The *Chicago Tribune* reported: "The dedicatory remarks by President Lincoln will live among the annals of man." Even the famous speaker Everett wrote Lincoln the next day to congratulate him. Everett said: "I should be glad, if I could flatter myself that I came as near to the central idea of the occasion, in two hours, as you did in two minutes."

Lincoln's prophetic speech not only focused the minds of Americans on the purpose behind the brutal Civil War, but became a text that future Americans, like Barack Obama, would return to again and again. Its words and message continue to help us find a way to understand and address our current struggles.

The Gettysburg Address

THURSDAY, NOVEMBER 19, 1863

FOURSCORE AND SEVEN YEARS AGO our fathers brought forth on this continent a new nation, conceived in liberty, and dedicated to the proposition that all men are created equal.

Now we are engaged in a great civil war, testing whether that nation, or any nation so conceived and so dedicated, can long endure. We are met on a great battlefield of that war. We have come to dedicate a portion of that field as a final resting-place for those who here gave their lives that this nation might live. It is altogether fitting and proper that we should do this.

But, in a larger sense, we cannot dedicate . . . we cannot consecrate . . . we cannot hallow . . . this ground. The brave men, living and dead, who struggled here, have consecrated it far above our poor power to add or detract. The world will little note nor long remember what we say here, but it can never forget what they did here. It is for us, the living, rather, to be dedicated here to the unfinished work which they who fought here have thus far so nobly advanced. It is rather for us to be here dedicated to the great task remaining before us . . . that from these honored dead we take increased devotion to that cause for which they gave the last full measure of devotion; that we here highly resolve that these dead shall not have died in vain; that this nation, under God, shall have a new birth of freedom; and that government of the people, by the people, for the people, shall not perish from the earth.

January 20, 2009: The Obama family waves to the crowd of over one million people assembled in Washington D.C. for Barack Obama's inauguration.

3.

Barack Obama

January 20, 2009: President Obama delivers his inaugural address to a crowd of over one million people gathered on the National Mall, the Washington Monument standing tall in front of him.

"That Great Gift of Freedom": Setting the Scene

THE WASHINGTON D.C. morning dawned partly cloudy and cold—temperatures under 20 degrees—as hundreds of thousands of people began gathering expectantly in the city. They came from every part of the United States and were mainly ordinary people. There was Rebecca Wilks, a forty-six-year-old woman with cerebral palsy whose friends raised $2,500 to send her to the inauguration: "Just pinch me," she told a reporter. There was Greg Weaver, the Amtrak conductor who had befriended Senator Joe Biden as Biden commuted from Wilmington, Delaware, to his office in Washington every day—and now Biden had invited Weaver and his wife to the inauguration. There was Chesley "Sully" Sullenberger, the pilot who had miraculously landed US Airways Flight 1549 in the Hudson River the week before, without loss of life, after the plane was hit by birds. President-elect Obama had invited him, his family, and the entire crew of 1549 to attend.

There were the members of high school and college marching bands from all over the country, including boys from the Bonnie Brae Residential Treatment Center in New Jersey, boys without homes to whom was attached, according to their director, "a long laundry list of negative labels." Yet because of their "pride and hope for the future," they had been picked to march in the inaugural parade that would come after Obama's swearing-in.

About a quarter of a million people with tickets—many of them picked through a lottery system—gathered near the west front of the Capitol Building. There were also the lucky sixteen hundred who would view the inauguration from seats on the specially erected platform. Hundreds of thousands more thronged the National Mall. People were cold. They had endured security precautions that had never before occurred at any inauguration. More than thirty-five thousand police officers, National Guardsmen, and plainclothes agents from more than fifty agencies were present. The spectators were not allowed to bring in any drinks or food items larger than a small snack. There was no place to sit in the mall and long lines for the portable bathrooms.

What had brought all these people together—and what had caused millions more to gather, in schools, homes, and workplaces, to watch the inaugural events on television and on the internet—was hope, hope embodied in the person of one man: Barack Obama, who was about to become the first African American president of the United States.

"It Better Be Good!"

As all these people gathered, Barack Obama and his wife, Michelle, attended services at St. John's Episcopal Church. St. John's is known as "the Church of the Presidents" because every president-elect since Franklin Roosevelt in 1933 has prayed there on the morning of his inauguration. Then he and Michelle went with Vice President–elect Joe Biden and his wife, Jill, to meet briefly with President George Bush and his wife, Laura, at the White House. After that, Bush and Obama rode together to the swearing-in ceremony, a ride that had become traditional since Martin Van Buren picked up outgoing president Andrew Jackson in 1837.

As he rode to the Capitol Building with Bush, it must have been hard for Barack Obama to keep from thinking about the speech he was going to make, one that so many people around the world were waiting to hear. He had spent days working on it, going through three different drafts to try to get the wording just right. The thought of Abraham Lincoln and his inspiring inaugural speeches was never far from Obama's mind. He knew that comparisons to the best inaugural speeches in our nation's history would be made, yet it was a challenge he was prepared to accept.

One night the previous week, Obama took Michelle and their daughters, Malia and Sasha, to the Lincoln Memorial, thrilling and startling some tourists who were surprised to see the president-elect show up just before closing time. Lincoln's second inaugural address is inscribed on the huge wall of the memorial. The speech is short—only 704 words long—and Barack Obama said after his visit: "I'm not sure whether [visiting the Lincoln Memorial] was wise, because every time you read that second inaugural, you start getting intimidated. . . . There is a genius to Lincoln that is not going to be matched."

Things weren't helped any when his daughter

Sasha asked if Obama's own speech was going to be that short, and his daughter Malia interrupted: "First African American president—it better be good."

"Havin' Some Fun, Making History"

Barack Obama said that his inauguration was a time for "havin' some fun, making history." The festivities began on the Saturday before the inauguration with Obama's symbolic train journey from Philadelphia to Washington, following part of the route Lincoln took. On Sunday evening came the big "We Are One" concert at the Lincoln Memorial, which was free to the public and featured such stars as Stevie Wonder, Bruce Springsteen, U2, Beyoncé, James Taylor, and folksinger Pete Seeger. Obama and his family were there, singing along and dancing. Malia snapped pictures with her digital camera.

Monday, the day before, was Martin Luther King Day, a national holiday. Many people thought the close juxtaposition of these two important days was fitting. "You have on the one hand Martin Luther King, Jr., as the beginning step in the civil rights movement," Louisiana Congressmen Anh Cao, the first Vietnamese American elected to the House of Representatives, told a reporter. "Then tomorrow you have President-elect Obama as the culmination of that movement."

Honoring the work of the civil rights leader, Barack Obama marked Martin Luther King Day as a "day of service." Obama visited wounded veterans at Walter Reed Army Hospital, then headed for a homeless shelter, where he grabbed a paint roller and began painting the walls. "We can't allow any idle hands," he said. "Everyone's got to be involved." And that night, Michelle Obama and Jill Biden hosted the Kids' Inaugural Ball. Featuring such stars as Miley Cyrus, the Jonas Brothers, Jamie Foxx, and Queen Latifah, it filled an auditorium with wildly cheering children of the families of Americans serving in the military. Michelle Obama told the kids present: "You guys are the future of this great nation."

"That Great Gift of Freedom"

When President-elect Obama arrived at the Capitol Building, he could see the awe-inspiring crowd awaiting him. While the temperature was still only 27 degrees, the sky was bright and sunny and the people cheerful and expectant. They were entertained by the music of the United States Marine Band and the San Francisco Boys' and Girls' Choruses. Soon dignitaries including former presidents Jimmy Carter, George H. W. Bush, and Bill Clinton, as well as soon-to-be-ex-President George Bush, began to file onto the reviewing stand.

First Vice President Biden was sworn in, and then came the moment everyone was waiting for. It was a little after noon. Michelle Obama held the Bible Abraham Lincoln was sworn in on at his first inaugural. Barack Obama placed his hand on it and repeated the words of the oath of office after Chief Justice of the Supreme Court John G. Roberts, Jr. There was a small glitch as Roberts accidentally put the word "faithfully" in the wrong spot in the oath, throwing off both men, but they made it through. After shaking hands with the chief justice and kissing Michelle, President Barack Obama approached the podium. A massive cheer arose from the crowd. Thousands of tiny American flags fluttered in the sunlight.

Many observers had pointed out in the weeks since Barack Obama was elected president that America was at a crossroads, as it had been when Abraham Lincoln was inaugurated, or when Franklin Roosevelt took office during the Great Depression. With almost his first words, Obama acknowledged this directly.

"Every so often the oath is taken amidst gathering

clouds and raging storms," he said. January 20, 2009, marked such a time. "Our nation is at war against a far-reaching network of violence and hatred. Our economy is badly weakened. . . . Homes have been lost, jobs shed, businesses shuttered."

Speaking in a loud, clear voice to the hundreds of thousands on the National Mall and the millions more at home and around the world, Obama said that there were those who felt that "America's decline is inevitable, that the next generation must lower its sights." But President Obama refused to accept this interpretation. "Starting today," he said, "we must pick ourselves up, dust ourselves off, and begin again the work of remaking America." We all need to work to help create jobs, make better schools, and find new sources of energy, he said—"harness the sun and the winds and the soil to fuel our cars and run our factories."

Obama cited the ideals of our Founding Fathers. He stressed that America remains a friend to all nations and peoples who seek a future of peace and dignity. He reminded those listening that the American spirit is strong and cannot be broken. He pointed to the strength of our patchwork heritage, saying, "We are a nation of Christians and Muslims, Jews and

Hindus, and nonbelievers. We are shaped by every language and culture, drawn from every end of this Earth." He noted that because America was able to emerge from a painful history of slavery, civil war, and segregation, the country "cannot help but believe that the old hatreds shall someday pass." The country's ability to overcome this difficult history gives it a special responsibility to usher in "a new era of peace" around the world, Obama argued.

It isn't going to be easy, he continued, but it's time for each and every American citizen to take the responsibility for the future in his or her hands. "We have duties to ourselves, our nation, and the world, duties that we do not grudgingly accept but rather seize gladly." Obama asked us to remember the inspiring words that George Washington, the father of the nation, shared during the most crucial moment of the Revolutionary War. When all seemed bleak and only hope and virtue could survive, Washington exhorted the patriots to find the courage to meet the challenges they faced. Obama asked Americans to face their challenges with the same spirit of bravery and hope.

It might seem a tall order, Obama admitted. He pointed out that sixty years ago, his father might not have been served in a restaurant in Washington D.C., simply because he was black. And now his son, Barack Hussein Obama, stood in this very city as president of the United States. If this was possible, all things, with hard work, imagination, and creativity, were possible as well. Freedom is something that every American is entitled to, something that is handed down from generation to generation, all the way back to the days of the Founding Fathers. Obama demanded that it be said of this generation that "we carried forth that great gift of freedom and delivered it safely to future generations."

When President Obama finished his inaugural speech, applause rang out, echoing up and down the streets and avenues of Washington. The inaugural parade was still to come. More than ten thousand people from all fifty states followed Barack Obama and Joe Biden on the one-and-a-half-mile parade route up Pennsylvania Avenue from the Capitol to the White House. That evening, there were ten official inaugural balls, and many more unofficial ones. But it was a phrase in the final sentence of the new president's speech—"that great gift of freedom"—that captured the true meaning of the inauguration of our first African American president.

President Obama's Inaugural Address

TUESDAY, JANUARY 20, 2009

MY FELLOW CITIZENS:

I stand here today humbled by the task before us, grateful for the trust you have bestowed, mindful of the sacrifices borne by our ancestors.

I thank President Bush for his service to our nation, as well as the generosity and cooperation he has shown throughout this transition.

Forty-four Americans have now taken the presidential oath.

The words have been spoken during rising tides of prosperity and the still waters of peace. Yet, every so often the oath is taken amidst gathering clouds and raging storms. At these moments, America has carried on not simply because of the skill or vision of those in high office, but because We the People have remained faithful to the ideals of our forbearers, and true to our founding documents.

So it has been. So it must be with this generation of Americans.

That we are in the midst of crisis is now well understood. Our nation is at war against a far-reaching network of violence and hatred. Our economy is badly weakened, a consequence of greed and irresponsibility on the part of some but also our collective failure to make hard choices and prepare the nation for a new age.

Homes have been lost, jobs shed, businesses shuttered. Our health care is too costly, our schools fail too many, and each day brings further evidence that the ways we use energy strengthen our adversaries and threaten our planet.

These are the indicators of crisis, subject to data and statistics. Less measurable, but no less profound, is a sapping of confidence across our land; a nagging fear that America's decline is inevitable, that the next generation must lower its sights.

Today I say to you that the challenges we face are real, they are serious and they are many. They will not be met easily or in a short span of time. But know this America: They will be met.

On this day, we gather because we have chosen hope over fear, unity of purpose over conflict and discord.

On this day, we come to proclaim an end to the petty grievances and false promises, the recriminations and worn-out dogmas that for far too long have strangled our politics.

We remain a young nation, but in the words of Scripture, the time has come to set aside childish things. The time has come to reaffirm our enduring spirit; to choose our better history; to carry forward that precious gift, that noble idea, passed on from generation to generation: the God-given promise that all are equal, all are free, and all deserve a chance to pursue their full measure of happiness.

In reaffirming the greatness of our nation, we understand that greatness is never a given. It must be earned. Our journey has never been one of shortcuts or settling for less.

It has not been the path for the faint-hearted, for those who prefer leisure over work, or seek only the pleasures of riches and fame.

Rather, it has been the risk-takers, the doers, the makers of things—some celebrated, but more often men and women obscure in their labor—who have carried us up the long, rugged path towards prosperity and freedom.

For us, they packed up their few worldly possessions and traveled across oceans in search of a new life. For us, they toiled in sweatshops and settled the West, endured the lash of the whip and plowed the hard earth.

For us, they fought and died in places Concord and Gettysburg; Normandy and Khe Sahn.

Time and again these men and women struggled and sacrificed and worked till their hands were raw so that we might live a better life. They saw America as bigger than the sum of our individual ambitions; greater than all the differences of birth or wealth or faction.

This is the journey we continue today. We remain the most prosperous, powerful nation on Earth. Our workers are no less productive than when this crisis began. Our minds are no less inventive, our goods and services no less needed than they were last week or last month or last year. Our capacity remains undiminished. But our time of standing pat, of protecting narrow interests and putting off unpleasant decisions—that time has surely passed.

Starting today, we must pick ourselves up, dust ourselves off, and begin again the work of remaking America.

For everywhere we look, there is work to be done.

The state of our economy calls for action: bold and swift. And we will act not only to create new jobs but to lay a new foundation for growth.

We will build the roads and bridges, the electric grids and digital lines that feed our commerce and bind us together.

We will restore science to its rightful place and wield technology's wonders to raise health care's quality and lower its costs.

We will harness the sun and the winds and the soil to fuel our cars and run our factories. And we will transform our schools and colleges and universities to meet the demands of a new age.

All this we can do. All this we will do.

Now, there are some who question the scale of our ambitions, who suggest that our system cannot tolerate too many big plans. Their memories are short, for they have forgotten what this country has already done, what free men and women can achieve when imagination is joined to common purpose and necessity to courage.

What the cynics fail to understand is that the ground has shifted beneath them, that the stale political arguments that have consumed us for so long, no longer apply.

The question we ask today is not whether our government is too big or too small, but whether it works, whether it helps families find jobs at a decent wage, care they can afford, a retirement that is dignified.

Where the answer is yes, we intend to move forward. Where the answer is no, programs will end.

And those of us who manage the public's

dollars will be held to account, to spend wisely, reform bad habits, and do our business in the light of day, because only then can we restore the vital trust between a people and their government.

Nor is the question before us whether the market is a force for good or ill. Its power to generate wealth and expand freedom is unmatched.

But this crisis has reminded us that without a watchful eye, the market can spin out of control. The nation cannot prosper long when it favors only the prosperous.

The success of our economy has always depended not just on the size of our gross domestic product, but on the reach of our prosperity; on the ability to extend opportunity to every willing heart—not out of charity, but because it is the surest route to our common good.

As for our common defense, we reject as

false the choice between our safety and our ideals.

Our founding fathers, faced with perils that we can scarcely imagine, drafted a charter to assure the rule of law and the rights of man, a charter expanded by the blood of generations.

Those ideals still light the world, and we will not give them up for expedience's sake.

And so, to all other peoples and governments who are watching today, from the grandest capitals to the small village where my father was born: know that America is a friend of each nation and every man, woman and child who seeks a future of peace and dignity, and we are ready to lead once more.

Recall that earlier generations faced down fascism and communism not just with missiles and tanks, but with the sturdy alliances and enduring convictions.

They understood that our power alone cannot protect us, nor does it entitle us to do as we please. Instead, they knew that our power grows through its prudent use. Our security emanates from the justness of our cause; the force of our example; the tempering qualities of humility and restraint.

We are the keepers of this legacy. Guided by these principles once more, we can meet those new threats that demand even greater effort, even greater cooperation and understanding between nations. We'll begin to responsibly leave Iraq to its people and forge a hard-earned peace in Afghanistan.

With old friends and former foes, we'll work tirelessly to lessen the nuclear threat and roll back the specter of a warming planet.

We will not apologize for our way of life nor will we waver in its defense.

And for those who seek to advance their aims by inducing terror and slaughtering innocents, we say to you now that our spirit is stronger and cannot be broken. You cannot outlast us, and we will defeat you.

For we know that our patchwork heritage is a strength, not a weakness.

We are a nation of Christians and Muslims, Jews and Hindus, and nonbelievers. We are shaped by every language and culture, drawn from every end of this Earth.

And because we have tasted the bitter swill of civil war and segregation and emerged from that dark chapter stronger and more united, we cannot help but believe that the old hatreds shall someday pass; that the lines of tribe shall soon dissolve; that as the world grows smaller, our common humanity shall reveal itself; and that America must play its role in ushering in a new era of peace.

To the Muslim world, we seek a new way forward, based on mutual interest and mutual respect.

To those leaders around the globe who seek to sow conflict or blame their society's ills on the West, know that your people will judge you on what you can build, not what you destroy.

To those who cling to power through corruption and deceit and the silencing of dissent, know that you are on the wrong side of history, but that we will extend a hand if you are willing to unclench your fist.

To the people of poor nations, we pledge to work alongside you to make your farms flourish and let clean waters flow; to nourish starved bodies and feed hungry minds.

And to those nations like ours that enjoy relative plenty, we say we can no longer afford indifference to the suffering outside our borders, nor can we consume the world's resources without regard to effect. For the world has changed, and we must change with it.

As we consider the road that unfolds before us, we remember with humble gratitude those brave Americans who, at this very hour, patrol far-off deserts and distant mountains. They have something to tell us, just as the fallen heroes who lie in Arlington whisper through the ages.

We honor them not only because they are guardians of our liberty, but because they embody the spirit of service: a willingness to find meaning in something greater than themselves.

And yet, at this moment, a moment that will define a generation, it is precisely this spirit that must inhabit us all.

For as much as government can do and must do, it is ultimately the faith and determination of the American people upon which this nation relies.

It is the kindness to take in a stranger when the levees break; the selflessness of workers who would rather cut their hours than see a friend lose their job which sees us through our darkest hours.

It is the firefighter's courage to storm a

stairway filled with smoke, but also a parent's willingness to nurture a child, that finally decides our fate.

Our challenges may be new, the instruments with which we meet them may be new, but those values upon which our success depends, honesty and hard work, courage and fair play, tolerance and curiosity, loyalty and patriotism—these things are old.

These things are true. They have been the quiet force of progress throughout our history.

What is demanded then is a return to these truths. What is required of us now is a new era of responsibility—a recognition, on the part of every American, that we have duties to ourselves, our nation and the world, duties that we do not grudgingly accept but rather seize gladly, firm in the knowledge that there is nothing so satisfying to the spirit, so defining of our character than giving our all to a difficult task.

This is the price and the promise of citizenship.

This is the source of our confidence: the knowledge that God calls on us to shape an uncertain destiny.

This is the meaning of our liberty and our creed, why men and women and children of every race and every faith can join in celebration across this magnificent mall. And why a man whose father less than sixty years ago might not have been served at a local restaurant can now stand before you to take a most sacred oath.

So let us mark this day in remembrance of who we are and how far we have traveled.

In the year of America's birth, in the coldest of months, a small band of patriots huddled by nine campfires on the shores of an icy river. The capital was abandoned. The enemy was advancing. The snow was stained with blood.

At a moment when the outcome of our

revolution was most in doubt, the father of our nation ordered these words be read to the people:

"Let it be told to the future world that in the depth of winter, when nothing but hope and virtue could survive, that the city and the country, alarmed at one common danger, came forth to meet it."

America, in the face of our common dangers, in this winter of our hardship, let us remember these timeless words; with hope and virtue, let us brave once more the icy currents, and endure what storms may come; let it be said by our children's children that when we were tested we refused to let this journey end, that we did not turn back nor did we falter; and with eyes fixed on the horizon and God's grace upon us, we carried forth that great gift of freedom and delivered it safely to future generations.

Thank you. God bless you.

And God bless the United States of America.

“We Are Not Enemies, But Friends”: Setting the Scene

ABRAHAM LINCOLN came to his first inauguration under conditions that no other president-elect has ever faced, before or since. For the ten years before 1861, the thirty-four states that made up America had been violently divided over the issue of whether the Southern states had the right to keep African Americans as slaves. As the country expanded westward, America argued about whether the new states being formed would be “slave” or “free” states.

Slave-holders in the South passionately hated Abraham Lincoln, because Lincoln believed that they did not have the right to create other slave-holding states. After Lincoln won the election of 1860, seven Southern states left the United States of America, followed by six others. They formed their own government, which they named the Confederate States of America. They even elected their own president, Jefferson Davis, and began raising an army. During this period, president-elect Lincoln was at his home in Springfield, Illinois, preparing himself for the awesome task of becoming president during such troubled times. He spent this time considering who he would appoint to his cabinet, and composing his inaugural address.

"I Have Got 4 Brothers"

Lincoln's law offices in Springfield were quickly filled with people who wanted him to help them get jobs. In order to find the privacy he needed to write his inaugural address, he had to go to a "dusty and neglected back room" above his brother-in-law's store. When Lincoln finished writing, he had a printer set the address in type on extra-long pages. There were seven pages. But as was his habit, Lincoln kept tinkering with his speech right up until the moment he gave it.

During this time in Springfield, the president-elect grew a beard. He most likely was inspired by a letter he received from an eleven-year-old girl from Westfield, New York, named Grace Bedell. Grace wrote Lincoln in October 1860, a month before the election: "I have got 4 brothers and part of them will vote for you any way and if you will let your whiskers grow I will try to get the rest of them to vote for you. You would look a great deal better, for your face is so thin. All the ladies like whiskers and they would tease their husbands to vote for you and then you would be president." Lincoln had never had a beard before, but when he left Springfield on February 11, 1861, bound for the White House, he was fully bearded. When the train stopped in Westfield on February 16, the president-elect appeared on the train platform and called out for Grace, who was in the crowd with her two sisters. She came forth, and Lincoln kissed her and told her he took her advice. And so, in all the pictures you see of Lincoln as president he has a beard.

As the train drew closer to Washington, the tension rose. There had been numerous threats to kill Lincoln. Because of the danger, he was guarded by detectives. At one point Lincoln was even made to wear a disguise of a plaid wool cap and an overcoat. Some newspapers mistook the overcoat for a garment borrowed from his wife, and others more seriously ridiculed the incumbent president for appearing cowardly. When he arrived in Washington, the city was full of rumors that "Lincoln will never be inaugurated; he will be shot before sundown."

On March 4, Lincoln rode to his swearing-in ceremony at the still-unfinished Capitol Building. Cavalry troopers closely flanked the president-elect's carriage, and people were barely able to see him. As Lincoln mounted the steps of the Capitol, one reporter captured his appearance: "He was tall and ungainly, wearing a black suit, a black tie beneath a turn-down collar and a black silk hat. He carried a gold or silver-headed walking cane."

"Great Presidents Face It"

In the nineteenth century most presidents made their inaugural addresses first, before taking the oath of office. This is the opposite of what happens today.

Lincoln stepped forward, opened his manuscript on the podium, and put his cane across it as a paperweight. For a moment he stared out over the crowd. There were those who said that the soon-to-be-sixteenth president of the United States did not have the experience to deal with this unprecedented situation. After all, the presidents who had come before him had been war heroes, great statesmen, and senators, or vice presidents who had learned about governing while in office. The only prior experience Lincoln had was his time in the Illinois state legislature, one two-year term in the United States Congress, and a successful law practice back home in Springfield. But, as the historian Matthew Pinsker has written: "Mediocre presidents run from bad news. Great presidents face it."

Speaking in a "high-pitched, but resonant" voice, Lincoln faced the issue of the divided state of the Union directly by devoting his entire speech to it. We think of Abraham Lincoln as the president who freed the slaves, so Lincoln's comments about slavery in his address are shocking. He said: "I have no purpose, directly or indirectly, to interfere with the institution of slavery in the States where it exists." Unlike more radical members of his party who wanted to end slavery as quickly as possible, Lincoln was intent on making compromises, even on slavery, in order to save the Union at all costs.

Lincoln believed that each state should have the freedom to control its own government exclusively, and that this principle was necessary for the United States to have a balance of power. Lincoln promised never to endanger the security of any part of the United States, and to protect every state equally under the Constitution.

Lincoln then addressed a particularly volatile issue that divided the country. The Fugitive Slave Act stated that any slave who escaped from one state to another had to be returned to his or her owner. Anyone who harbored a fugitive—or runaway—slave was breaking the law. Surrounding this issue was the question of who should enforce this law—the federal government or the individual states. Many people, especially in the Northern states, were abolitionists. They believed that slavery was wrong and should be outlawed, and were not diligent in enforcing the Fugitive Slave Act.

To any who felt certain laws were wrong, Lincoln stressed the importance of invoking change through legal actions and amendments. Disregarding laws, he argued, would only bring about violence and instability.

Then Lincoln focused on the history of the United States—that power was transferred from president to president peacefully, and that the people were in control. He pointed out that these were unprecedented times. No state had ever before attempted to formally secede from the federal union. He argued that no government ever provides for its own destruction and that, therefore, secession was unconstitutional.

"The Union of These States Is Perpetual"

Using his background as a lawyer and drawing on his study of the United States Constitution, Lincoln made a legal argument for keeping the Union sound. "I hold that . . . the Union of these States is perpetual," he declared, meaning that the United States was meant to go on forever. Indeed, one of the main goals of the Constitution is expressed in the statement at the beginning of the document: "To form a more perfect Union." Would breaking apart the Union, as the Confederacy intended to do, further that goal? Obviously not. Therefore, it would be Lincoln's Constitutional duty as president to hold the United States together. "And I shall perform it," Lincoln cried, drawing loud applause.

Lincoln cited the impressive history of the nation, and the original idea of the Union. He inspired his audience by describing the ideals of the founding fathers. The Union was the principle America was founded upon, older than the Constitution itself. It was created by the Articles of Association in 1774 and expanded upon by the Declaration of Independence in 1776, and was intended to endure forever by the thirteen states that created the Articles of Confederation in 1778. Since the lawful preservation of the Union was the basis of the Constitution, Lincoln maintained that it was illegal and revolutionary for any state to act against the authority of the United States as a whole.

Lincoln hoped that a peaceful solution could be reached and did not want to use force or bloodshed to keep the Union together. He reminded those states that might wish to secede that America had a rich history, filled with hope and promise. He asked them to consider all the benefits of being a part of a truly free and democratic country before rashly deciding to break apart from it. He promised that the federal government would continue to offer security to all the citizens of the United States. With this security of the government, peace and stability would endure.

Part of Lincoln's argument was that the Constitution, as a set of ideals, could never cover every possible real-life scenario. It was not expressly written whether slavery should be prohibited or protected. Though the Constitution might be open to interpretation, its ideals had to be upheld. Lincoln reminded the nation that it was up to the people to make these interpretations. But he also warned that a government controlled by the people meant that the majority must rule. The beauty of American democracy was that the government remained changeable along with the views of its people. He felt that secession of a minority who disagreed with the views generally held by the rest of the country was the same as anarchy, or chaos.

Lincoln spoke passionately of preserving the Union, of bridging the divide. He pointed out that "one section of our country believes slavery is right and ought to be extended, while the other believes it is wrong and ought not be extended." He compared the situation between the North and the South to a troubled marriage. "A husband and wife may be divorced and go out of the presence and beyond the reach of each other," he said, "but the different parts of our country can not do this."

"The Momentous Issue of Civil War"

Lincoln appealed to the people as one of them, as their fellow citizen, and put the power in their hands. The country and its laws belonged to them. The Union and its government were a part of them. He asked that they have confidence in the government that they, the people, had put in place. He referred to the sense of continuity represented by the inaugural ceremony and the change of power every four years.

Lincoln reminded Southern secessionists that "the momentous issue of civil war" was "in your hands . . . and not in mine." In an early draft of the speech, Lincoln ended with a challenge: "Shall it be peace or a sword?" But he had been convinced by Secretary of State William H. Seward that he needed to add "some final words of affection, some of calm and cheerful confidence." Therefore, Lincoln decided to conclude his first inaugural address with a plea for harmony: "We are not enemies, but friends," he said. "We must not be enemies. Though passion may have strained it must not break our bonds of affection."

Lincoln then took the oath of office from eighty-four-year-old Chief Justice Roger Taney. Taney was the Supreme Court judge who had written the majority opinion in an important case called *Dred Scott v. Sanford.* This ruling held that African Americans were not citizens of the United States, and that the federal government did not have the authority to outlaw slavery in any state or in new territories as the country expanded. Lincoln opposed the ruling, and he urged that it be overturned through the legal process. While this helped build support for Lincoln in the North, it also enraged those, like Taney, who favored slavery. Onlookers said that as he swore in Lincoln as president, Taney "trembled uncontrollably and looked like a galvanized corpse."

Unfortunately, Lincoln's plea for compromise and friendship with the South would fall on deaf ears. Within a month, the first shots of the Civil War were fired.

President Lincoln's First Inaugural Address

MONDAY, MARCH 4, 1861

FELLOW-CITIZENS OF THE UNITED STATES:

In compliance with a custom as old as the Government itself, I appear before you to address you briefly and to take in your presence the oath prescribed by the Constitution of the United States to be taken by the President before he enters on the execution of this office.

I do not consider it necessary at present for me to discuss those matters of administration about which there is no special anxiety or excitement.

Apprehension seems to exist among the people of the Southern States that by the accession of a Republican Administration their property and their peace and personal security are to be endangered. There has never been any reasonable cause for such apprehension. Indeed, the most ample evidence to the contrary has all the while existed and been open to their inspection. It is found in nearly all the published speeches of him who now addresses you. I do but quote from one of those speeches when I declare that—I have no purpose, directly or indirectly, to interfere with the institution of slavery in the States where it exists. I believe I have no lawful right to do so, and I have no inclination to do so.

Those who nominated and elected me did so with full knowledge that I had made this and many similar declarations and had never recanted them; and more than this, they placed in the platform for my acceptance, and as a law to themselves and to me, the clear and emphatic resolution which I now read:

Resolved, That the maintenance inviolate of the rights of the States, and especially the right of each State to order and control its own domestic institutions according to its own judgment exclusively, is essential to that balance of power on which the perfection and endurance of our political fabric depend; and we denounce the lawless invasion by armed force of the soil of any State or Territory, no matter what pretext, as among the gravest of crimes.

I now reiterate these sentiments, and in doing so I only press upon the public attention the most conclusive evidence of which the case is susceptible that the property, peace, and security of no section are to be in any wise endangered by the now incoming Administration. I add, too, that all the protection which, consistently with the Constitution and the laws, can be given will be cheerfully given to all the States when lawfully demanded, for whatever cause—as cheerfully to one section as to another.

There is much controversy about the delivering up of fugitives from service or labor. The clause I now read is as plainly written in the Constitution as any other of its provisions: No person held to service or labor in one State, under the laws thereof, escaping into another, shall in consequence of any law or regulation therein be discharged from such service or labor, but shall be delivered up on claim of the party to whom such service or labor may be due.

It is scarcely questioned that this provision was intended by those who made it for the reclaiming of what we call fugitive slaves; and the intention of the lawgiver is the law. All members of Congress swear their support to the whole Constitution—to this provision as much as to any other. To the proposition, then, that slaves whose cases come within the terms of this clause "shall be delivered up" their oaths are unanimous. Now, if they would make the effort in good temper, could they not with nearly equal unanimity frame and pass a law by means of which to keep good that unanimous oath?

There is some difference of opinion whether this clause should be enforced by national or by State authority, but surely that difference is not a very material one. If the slave is to be surrendered, it can be of but little consequence to him or to others by which authority it is done. And should anyone in any case be content that his oath shall go unkept on a merely unsubstantial controversy as to how it shall be kept?

Again: In any law upon this subject ought not all the safeguards of liberty known in civilized and humane jurisprudence to be introduced, so that a free man be not in any case surrendered as a slave? And might it not be well at the same time to provide by law for the enforcement of that clause in the Constitution which guarantees that "the citizens of each State shall be entitled to all privileges and immunities of citizens in the several States"?

I take the official oath today with no mental reservations and with no purpose to construe the Constitution or laws by any hypercritical rules; and while I do not choose now to specify particular acts of Congress as proper to be enforced, I do suggest that it will be much safer for all, both in official and private stations, to conform to and abide by all those acts which stand unrepealed than to violate any of them trusting to find impunity in having them held to be unconstitutional.

It is seventy-two years since the first inauguration of a President under our National Constitution. During that period fifteen different and greatly distinguished citizens have in succession administered the executive branch of the Government. They have conducted it through many perils, and generally with great success. Yet, with all this scope of precedent, I now enter upon the same task for the brief constitutional term of four years under great and peculiar difficulty. A disruption of the Federal Union, heretofore only menaced, is now formidably attempted.

I hold that in contemplation of universal law and of the Constitution the Union of these States is perpetual. Perpetuity is implied, if not expressed, in the fundamental law of all national governments. It is safe to assert that no government proper ever had a provision in its organic law for its own termination. Continue to execute all the express provisions of our National Constitution, and the Union will endure forever, it being impossible to destroy it except by some action not provided for in the instrument itself.

Again: If the United States be not a government proper, but an association of States in the nature of contract merely, can it, as a contract, be peaceably unmade by less than all the parties who made it? One party to a contract may violate it—break it, so to speak—but does it not require all to lawfully rescind it?

Descending from these general principles, we find the proposition that in legal contemplation the Union is perpetual confirmed by the history of the Union itself. The Union is much older than the Constitution. It was formed, in fact, by the Articles of Association in 1774. It was matured and continued by the Declaration of Independence in 1776. It was further matured, and the faith of all the then thirteen States expressly plighted and engaged that it should be perpetual, by the Articles of Confederation in 1778. And finally, in 1787, one of the declared objects for ordaining and establishing the Constitution was "to form a more perfect Union."

But if destruction of the Union by one or by a part only of the States be lawfully possible, the Union is less perfect than before the Constitution, having lost the vital element of perpetuity.

It follows from these views that no State upon its own mere motion can lawfully get out of the Union; that resolves and ordinances to that effect are legally void, and that acts of violence within any State or States against the authority of the United States are insurrectionary or revolutionary, according to circumstances.

I therefore consider that in view of the Constitution and the laws the Union is unbroken, and to the extent of my ability, I shall take care, as the Constitution itself expressly enjoins upon me, that the laws of the Union be faithfully executed in all the States. Doing this I deem to be only a simple duty on my part, and

I shall perform it so far as practicable unless my rightful masters, the American people, shall withhold the requisite means or in some authoritative manner direct the contrary. I trust this will not be regarded as a menace, but only as the declared purpose of the Union that it will constitutionally defend and maintain itself.

In doing this there needs to be no bloodshed or violence, and there shall be none unless it be forced upon the national authority. The power confided to me will be used to hold, occupy, and possess the property and places belonging to the Government and to collect the duties and imposts; but beyond what may be necessary for these objects, there will be no invasion, no using of force against or among the people anywhere. Where hostility to the United States in any interior locality shall be so great and universal as to prevent competent resident citizens from holding the Federal offices, there will be no attempt to force obnoxious strangers among the people for that object. While the strict legal right may exist in the Government to enforce the exercise of these offices, the attempt to do so would be so irritating and so nearly impracticable withal that I deem it better to forego for the time the uses of such offices.

The mails, unless repelled, will continue to be furnished in all parts of the Union. So far as possible the people everywhere shall have that sense of perfect security which is most favorable to calm thought and reflection. The course here indicated will be followed unless current events and experience shall show a modification or change to be proper, and in every case and exigency my best discretion will be exercised, according to circumstances actually existing and with a view and a hope of a peaceful solution of the national troubles and the restoration of fraternal sympathies and affections.

That there are persons in one section or another who seek to destroy the Union at all events and are glad of any pretext to do it I will neither affirm nor deny; but if there be such, I need address no word to them. To those, however, who really love the Union may I not speak?

Before entering upon so grave a matter as the destruction of our national fabric, with all its benefits, its memories, and its hopes, would it not be wise to ascertain precisely why we do it? Will you hazard so desperate a step while there is any possibility that any portion of the ills you fly from have no real existence? Will you, while the certain ills you fly to are greater than all the real ones you fly from, will you risk the commission of so fearful a mistake?

All profess to be content in the Union if all constitutional rights can be maintained. Is it true, then, that any right plainly written in the Constitution has been denied? I think not.

Happily, the human mind is so constituted that no party can reach to the audacity of doing this. Think, if you can, of a single instance in which a plainly written provision of the Constitution has ever been denied. If by the mere force of numbers a majority should deprive a minority of any clearly written constitutional right, it might in a moral point of view justify revolution; certainly would if such right were a vital one. But such is not our case. All the vital rights of minorities and of individuals are so plainly assured to them by affirmations and negations, guaranties and prohibitions, in the Constitution that controversies never arise concerning them. But no organic law can ever be framed with a provision specifically applicable to every question which may occur in practical administration. No foresight can anticipate nor any document of reasonable length contain express provisions for all possible questions. Shall fugitives from labor be surrendered by national or by State authority? The Constitution does not expressly say. May Congress prohibit slavery in the Territories? The Constitution does not expressly say. Must Congress protect slavery in the Territories? The Constitution does not expressly say.

From questions of this class spring all our constitutional controversies, and we divide upon them into majorities and minorities. If the minority will not acquiesce, the majority must, or the Government must cease. There is no other alternative, for continuing the Government is acquiescence on one side or the other. If a minority in such case will secede rather than acquiesce, they make a precedent which in turn will divide and ruin them, for a minority of their own will secede from them whenever a majority refuses to be controlled by such minority. For instance, why may not any portion of a new confederacy a year or two hence arbitrarily secede again, precisely as portions of the present Union now claim to secede from it? All who cherish disunion sentiments are now being educated to the exact temper of doing this.

Is there such perfect identity of interests among the States to compose a new union as to produce harmony only and prevent renewed secession?

Plainly the central idea of secession is the essence of anarchy. A majority held in restraint by constitutional checks and limitations, and always changing easily with deliberate changes of popular opinions and sentiments, is the only true sovereign of a free people. Whoever rejects it does of necessity fly to anarchy or to despotism. Unanimity is impossible. The rule of a minority, as a permanent arrangement, is wholly inadmissible; so that, rejecting the majority principle, anarchy or despotism in some form is all that is left.

I do not forget the position assumed by

some that constitutional questions are to be decided by the Supreme Court, nor do I deny that such decisions must be binding in any case upon the parties to a suit as to the object of that suit, while they are also entitled to very high respect and consideration in all parallel cases by all other departments of the Government. And while it is obviously possible that such decision may be erroneous in any given case, still the evil effect following it, being limited to that particular case, with the chance that it may be overruled and never become a precedent for other cases, can better be borne than could the evils of a different practice. At the same time, the candid citizen must confess that if the policy of the Government upon vital questions affecting the whole people is to be irrevocably fixed by decisions of the Supreme Court, the instant they are made in ordinary litigation between parties in personal actions the people will have ceased to be their own rulers, having to that extent practically resigned their Government into the hands of that eminent tribunal. Nor is there in this view any assault upon the court or the judges. It is a duty from which they may not shrink to decide cases properly brought before them, and it is no fault of theirs if others seek to turn their decisions to political purposes.

One section of our country believes slavery is right and ought to be extended, while the other believes it is wrong and ought not to be extended. This is the only substantial dispute. The fugitive-slave clause of the Constitution and the law for the suppression of the foreign slave trade are each as well enforced, perhaps, as any law can ever be in a community where the moral sense of the people imperfectly supports the law itself. The great body of the people abide by the dry legal obligation in both cases, and a few break over in each. This, I think, can not be perfectly cured, and it would be worse in both cases after the separation of the sections than before. The foreign slave trade, now imperfectly suppressed, would be ultimately revived without restriction in one section, while fugitive slaves, now only partially surrendered, would not be surrendered at all by the other.

Physically speaking, we can not separate. We can not remove our respective sections from each other nor build an impassable wall between them. A husband and wife may be divorced and go out of the presence and beyond the reach of each other, but the different parts of our country can not do this. They can not but remain face to face, and intercourse, either amicable or hostile, must continue between them. Is it possible, then, to make that intercourse more advantageous or more satisfactory after separation than before? Can aliens make treaties easier than friends can make laws? Can treaties be more faithfully enforced between aliens than laws can among friends? Suppose you go to war, you can not fight always; and when, after much loss on both sides and no gain on either, you cease fighting, the identical old questions, as to terms of intercourse, are again upon you.

This country, with its institutions, belongs to the people who inhabit it. Whenever they shall grow weary of the existing Government, they can exercise their constitutional right of amending it or their revolutionary right to dismember or overthrow it. I can not be ignorant of the fact that many worthy and patriotic citizens are desirous of having the National Constitution amended. While I make no recommendation of amendments, I fully recognize the rightful authority of the people over the whole subject, to be exercised in either of the modes prescribed in the instrument itself; and I should, under existing circumstances, favor rather than oppose a fair opportunity being afforded the people to act upon it. I will venture to add that to me the convention mode seems preferable, in that it allows amendments to originate with the people themselves, instead of only permitting them to take or reject propositions originated by others, not especially chosen for the purpose, and which might not be precisely such as they would wish to either accept or refuse. I understand a proposed amendment to the Constitution—which amendment, however, I have not seen—has passed Congress, to the effect that the Federal Government shall never interfere with the domestic institutions of the States, including that of persons held to service. To avoid misconstruction of what I have said, I depart from my purpose not to speak of particular amendments so far as to say that, holding such a provision to now be implied constitutional law, I have no objection to its being made express and irrevocable.

The Chief Magistrate derives all his authority from the people, and they have referred none upon him to fix terms for the separation of the States. The people themselves can do this if also they choose, but the Executive as such has nothing to do with it. His duty is to administer the present Government as it came to his hands and to transmit it unimpaired by him to his successor.

Why should there not be a patient confidence in the ultimate justice of the people? Is there any better or equal hope in the world? In our present differences, is either party without faith of being in the right? If the Almighty Ruler of Nations, with His eternal truth and justice, be on your side of the North, or on yours of the South, that truth and that justice will surely prevail by the judgment of this great tribunal of the American people.

By the frame of the Government under which we live this same people have wisely given their public servants but little power for mischief, and have with equal wisdom provided for the return of that little to their own hands at very short intervals. While the people retain their virtue and vigilance no Administration by any extreme of wickedness or folly can very seriously injure the Government in the short space of four years.

My countrymen, one and all, think calmly and well upon this whole subject. Nothing valuable can be lost by taking time. If there be an object to hurry any of you in hot haste to a step which you would never take deliberately, that object will be frustrated by taking time; but no good object can be frustrated by it. Such of you as are now dissatisfied still have the old Constitution unimpaired, and, on the sensitive point, the laws of your own framing under it; while the new Administration will have no immediate power, if it would, to change either. If it were admitted that you who are dissatisfied hold the right side in the dispute, there still is no single good reason for precipitate action. Intelligence, patriotism, Christianity, and a firm reliance on Him who has never yet forsaken this favored land are still competent to adjust in the best way all our present difficulty.

In your hands, my dissatisfied fellow-countrymen, and not in mine, is the momentous issue of civil war. The Government will not assail you. You can have no conflict without being yourselves the aggressors. You have no oath registered in heaven to destroy the Government, while I shall have the most solemn one to "preserve, protect, and defend it."

I am loath to close. We are not enemies, but friends. We must not be enemies. Though passion may have strained it must not break our bonds of affection. The mystic chords of memory, stretching from every battlefield and patriot grave to every living heart and hearthstone all over this broad land, will yet swell the chorus of the Union, when again touched, as surely they will be, by the better angels of our nature.

"With Malice Toward None, with Charity for All": Setting the Scene

A GREAT DEAL HAD CHANGED in the time between Abraham Lincoln's first inaugural address and his second, which was given on March 4, 1865.

The bloodiest war in American history was just coming to a close, with a staggering cost of a total of 620,000 dead. On January 1, 1863, Lincoln had issued his famous Emancipation Proclamation, which freed all slaves in any area outside Union control. He had won reelection to the presidency in November, beating his opponent by some four hundred thousand votes. Since the Confederate States of America did not vote, only a little over four million votes were cast, so Lincoln won by ten percent of the vote. And now the North was about to win the war. In just over a month's time, on April 9, General Robert E. Lee would surrender his Army of Virginia to Ulysses S. Grant at Appomattox Courthouse in Virginia.

Lincoln himself had changed significantly. In his first inaugural address, he had been entirely focused on keeping the country together at all costs. He had been so concerned, in fact, that he was willing to allow the Southern states to keep their slaves, as long as they did not withdraw from the Union. But now, four long and savage years of war, the urgings of abolitionists—those who wanted to get rid of slavery completely—and his own profound thoughts on the matter had changed Abraham Lincoln's mind.

He began writing his second inaugural address in February 1865. From the beginning he knew it was something special. In late February, about a week before the inauguration, Lincoln carried the manuscript into his office, holding it under his arm. He told a few friends who were there: "Lots of wisdom in that document, I suspect. It is what will be called my 'second inaugural,' containing about six hundred words. I will put it away in this drawer until I want it."

Lincoln put the speech in his desk and walked away. His words and actions expressed a hard-won confidence in his ability to write and convey his ideas. He now had a much stronger belief in himself and his abilities than he did when he was writing his first inaugural address.

Gloomy Weather

March 4 fell on a Saturday in 1865. The morning was gloomy and rain was falling steadily, so much so that mud seeped up through the pavement bricks. In those days, paved streets were made of brick or cobblestone, not covered with cement or asphalt. The seeping mud made a mess of everyone's shoes and the long, trailing dresses of the women spectators. Although the rain stopped falling before the ceremony, everyone waiting had gotten a good soaking.

But this inauguration day was different from the last. The mood of the crowd was far less tense. And, during the usual procession to the Capitol Building, African Americans—Union soldiers—had marched for the very first time in an inaugural parade.

Once he arrived at the Capitol, Lincoln delivered his speech with great confidence, in his unique voice. Although everyone in the large crowd could hear him, his voice was not particularly loud, but instead high and clear "with almost a metallic ring," according to one spectator.

Lincoln's second inaugural address was one of the shortest inaugural addresses ever made—four paragraphs and just under seven hundred words.

The president began by saying that "the progress of our arms"—meaning how well the Union armies had been doing—was "well-known [and] reasonably satisfactory and encouraging." But he was not going to congratulate himself or the people of the North on how well the war was going. He wanted to talk about something else. He reminded his listeners that, when he gave his first inaugural address in 1861, it was "devoted altogether to saving the Union without war." And yet, even as he had made that speech, there had been those seeking to destroy the Union. Thus, Lincoln said, "war came."

The war was far longer and bloodier than either side ever imagined it would be. Both sides called on God to help them win it. But, Lincoln then said, the South did something very different: "It may seem strange that any man should dare to ask a just God's assistance in wringing their bread from the sweat of other men's faces."

In other words, the South had asked God to help them win a war so that they might be able to continue to make people slaves. And no matter how terrible a war or how divided the Union might become, Abraham Lincoln was no longer willing to accept this. "American slavery," he said, needed to come to an end, even if "God wills that [the war] continue until . . . every drop of blood drawn with the lash shall be paid by another drawn with the sword."

Lincoln meant that God's justice would be brought against each person who had harmed a slave, if that was what it took to make the South surrender. This was an important statement, for while the South was losing the war, there were many there who did not want to give up. Lincoln was telling them that they must, or else lose all.

"Did You Notice That Sunburst?"

Lincoln ended the speech on a much kindlier note. He knew that there were many in the North who wanted to punish the South severely for its actions, even beyond the punishment that had occurred during the war. But Lincoln did not agree with that view. In the final lines of his second inaugural address—among the most famous inaugural lines in American history—he said:

"With malice toward none, with charity for all,

with firmness in the right as God gives us to see the right, let us strive on to finish the work we are in, to bind up the nation's wounds, to care for him who shall have borne the battle and for his widow and his orphan, to do all which may achieve and cherish a just and lasting peace among ourselves and with all nations."

When the speech ended, the reporter Noah Brooks wrote, there was "a profound silence." Many people were crying. The new chief justice of the Supreme Court, Salmon P. Chase, then brought out a Bible and gave the oath of office to Lincoln. And just at that moment, almost like a scene from a movie, the sun came out and a shaft of light shone down on the president. Afterward, an excited Lincoln said to the reporter Brooks: "Did you notice that sunburst? It made my heart jump."

Unfortunately, another person at the inauguration noticed that sunburst, and it did not make him happy. That was John Wilkes Booth, the man who would shoot Abraham Lincoln in Ford's Theatre on April 14, some five weeks later. Historians have identified Booth in photographs of the inauguration. It is a sad thing to think that even at the moment Abraham Lincoln had grown to become one of our greatest presidents, his future assassin was staring him down and plotting to kill him.

Despite John Wilkes Booth's actions, Lincoln lives on in the hearts and minds of Americans. His second inaugural address, especially, is treasured. It is inscribed on the walls of the Lincoln Memorial in Washington D.C. The monument was completed in 1922 and is visited by millions of Americans every year. In 1963, Martin Luther King gave his famous "I Have a Dream" civil rights speech from the steps of the Lincoln Memorial. And since 1981, every president-elect, including Barack Obama, has taken his oath of office on the west front of the Capitol Building, from which he can see in the distance across the National Mall the glory of the Lincoln Memorial.

National Photo Company Collection, Prints & Photographs Division, Library of Congress, LC-USZ62-2578

March 4, 1865: Lincoln is sworn in at his second inauguration.

President Lincoln's Second Inaugural Address

SATURDAY, MARCH 4, 1865

FELLOW-COUNTRYMEN:

At this second appearing to take the oath of the Presidential office there is less occasion for an extended address than there was at the first. Then a statement somewhat in detail of a course to be pursued seemed fitting and proper. Now, at the expiration of four years, during which public declarations have been constantly called forth on every point and phase of the great contest which still absorbs the attention and engrosses the energies of the nation, little that is new could be presented.

The progress of our arms, upon which all else chiefly depends, is as well known to the public as to myself, and it is, I trust, reasonably satisfactory and encouraging to all. With high hope for the future, no prediction in regard to it is ventured.

On the occasion corresponding to this four years ago all thoughts were anxiously directed to an impending civil war. All dreaded it, all sought to avert it. While the inaugural address was being delivered from this place, devoted altogether to saving the Union without war, insurgent agents were in the city seeking to destroy it without war—seeking to dissolve the Union and divide effects by negotiation. Both parties deprecated war, but one of them would make war rather than let the nation survive, and the other would accept war rather than let it perish, and the war came.

One-eighth of the whole population were colored slaves, not distributed generally over the Union, but localized in the southern part of it. These slaves constituted a peculiar and powerful interest. All knew that this interest was somehow the cause of the war. To strengthen, perpetuate, and extend this interest was the object for which the insurgents would rend the Union even by war, while the Government claimed no right to do more than to restrict the territorial enlargement of it. Neither party expected for the war the magnitude or the duration which it has already attained. Neither anticipated that the cause of the conflict might cease with or even before the conflict itself should cease. Each looked for an easier triumph and a result less fundamental and astounding. Both read the same Bible and pray to the same God, and each invokes His aid against the other. It may seem strange that any men should dare to ask a just God's assistance in wringing their bread from the sweat of other men's faces, but let us judge not, that we be not judged. The prayers of both could not be answered. That of neither has been answered fully. The Almighty has His own purposes. "Woe unto the world because of offenses; for it must needs be that offenses come, but woe to that man by whom the offense cometh." If we shall suppose that American slavery is one of those offenses which, in the providence of God, must needs come, but which, having continued through His appointed time, He now wills to remove, and that He gives to both North and South this terrible war as the woe due to those by whom the offense came, shall we discern therein any departure from those divine attributes which the believers in a living God always ascribe to Him? Fondly do we hope, fervently do we pray, that this mighty scourge of war may speedily pass away. Yet, if God wills that it continue until all the wealth piled by the bondsman's two hundred and fifty years of unrequited toil shall be sunk, and until every drop of blood drawn with the lash shall be paid by another drawn with the sword, as was said three thousand years ago, so still it must be said "the judgments of the Lord are true and righteous altogether."

With malice toward none, with charity for all, with firmness in the right as God gives us to see the right, let us strive on to finish the work we are in, to bind up the nation's wounds, to care for him who shall have borne the battle and for his widow and his orphan, to do all which may achieve and cherish a just and lasting peace among ourselves and with all nations.

January 20, 2009: President Obama waves to the cheering crowd assembled to hear his speech on inauguration day.

5.

Two Senators from Illinois

Introducing Abraham Lincoln

If you happened to live in the town of Springfield, Illinois, in the 1840s and met Abraham Lincoln—this was well before he became famous—you would probably never be able to forget him. He was six feet four inches tall at a time when the average man was about five feet seven inches tall. He weighed 180 pounds, which made him very skinny. The historian Stephen B. Oates has written that Lincoln's height was "all in his legs. When he was sitting, he was no taller than the average man; but when he stood, he kept rising until he towered over his friends as though he was standing on stilts."

He was a friendly man and loved to tell stories. Yet in some ways he was a very private person. William Herndon, the law partner who had known him for thirty years, said that Lincoln "was hidden and liked to keep his own secrets."

"A Hunt After an Idea"

One reason that Lincoln may have seemed "hidden" to people is that he spent a lot of time by himself thinking about things. Lincoln, despite his humor, took things seriously.

"I remember how, when a mere child, I used to get irritated when anybody talked to me in a way I could not understand," Lincoln once told a friend. Late at night, listening to grown-ups having conversations downstairs, the young Lincoln paced the floor in his bedroom until he figured out what they were talking about. "I could not sleep . . . I got on such a hunt after an idea, until I had caught it."

Lincoln was born on February 12, 1809, in a one-room cabin in backwoods Kentucky. His father was Thomas Lincoln, a farmer and skilled carpenter. His mother, Nancy Hanks, took care of the family. Lincoln's ancestry and early life was marked by many sad events. His grandfather, after whom he was named, was killed by Indians in 1786. His brother, Thomas, born when Lincoln was three, died of an illness.

Then, when Lincoln was nine, in 1818, his mother died. During this time, Lincoln's father was often absent looking for work and Lincoln and his older sister, Sarah, were taken care of by a distant cousin. They often did not have enough to eat or proper clothes to wear.

Lincoln's mother and brother, his sister, and later two of his own sons died of illnesses that would be curable today. In some ways, this made him melancholy and sad, but it also toughened him and helped him speak genuinely to the American people when they suffered great losses in the war.

"The Best Boy That Ever Was"

After his wife's death, Thomas Lincoln moved the family to a farm in Indiana where they lived in better circumstances. He married again in 1819. Lincoln grew to love his stepmother, Sarah Bush Lincoln, very much, and she called him "the best boy that ever was."

During his childhood, Lincoln attended school for only about a year in total. Most of the time he had to work in the fields. The schools in frontier Kentucky and Indiana were known as "blab" schools because students learned by "blabbing" (or repeating) lessons aloud over and over again until they had memorized them.

Although there is a legend that Lincoln studied by the fireplace of his family's one-room log cabin, the entire family slept in front of the fireplace, so he probably had to go to sleep at the same time as they did. But he did later tell of reading while he was plowing behind a horse—Lincoln read the Bible and tales of adventure like *Robinson Crusoe.*

In 1830, when Lincoln was twenty-one years old, his father moved the family again, this time to a farm near the town of Decatur, Illinois, on the Sangamon River. Lincoln was now fully grown and wanted more out of life than farming. He became a clerk in a grocery store in the town of New Salem, Illinois. He would work all day and read in his tiny room in the back of the store at night. There he explored the work of William Shakespeare and the poet Lord Byron, as well as the United States Constitution and books on the American Revolution.

Although Lincoln was a tall, awkward young man with messy black hair and pants that didn't even reach down to his ankles, he was ambitious. Two years after arriving in town with nothing in his pocket, he ran for the Illinois General Assembly, the state legislature that passes the laws that govern Illinois. He lost. Then a short-lived Indian war broke out and Lincoln was voted by his fellow townspeople as captain of the militia. He spent three months wandering around the woods. He saw no fighting but had, as he said with his characteristic good humor, "a good many struggles with musketoes [mosquitoes]." Two years later, he ran for the Illinois General Assembly again. This time he won.

"Honest Abe"

Since his job as a representative was part-time, he was able to study for and receive a law degree while he served. He fell in love and married a woman named Mary Todd in November of 1842. And in 1846, Lincoln was elected to the United States House of Representatives, which, along with the United States Senate, passes the laws that govern our land.

After 1849, Lincoln left Congress to work full-time as a lawyer, traveling around Illinois defending those accused of wrongdoing. He began to be called "Honest Abe" because of his fair dealings with people. In the 1850s, Lincoln joined the new Republican Party. He began to speak out against slavery and against the growing idea, in the South, that it could withdraw from the Union and form its own country. In 1858, Lincoln ran for senator from Illinois against a man named Stephen A. Douglas. Lincoln gave a famous speech in which he told his audience that "a house divided against itself cannot stand"—in other words, he warned that America could not survive being torn in half if the South withdrew from the country.

Lincoln lost the Senate race to Douglas but become known nationwide during a series of seven debates that he had with Douglas about national issues, especially slavery. His intelligence and passion were admired, as well as his sense of humor. Once, when Douglas accused him of being "two-faced," Lincoln replied: "If I had another face, do you think I'd wear this one?"

Slavery and the future of the United States were the key issues of the time. The country was divided between "free states" and "slave states." Most of the Northern states that had once allowed slavery no longer did so. In most of the Southern states, the number of slaves was larger than ever, and the economy relied on their labor. There were about four million African American slaves in America out of a total population of twenty-seven million people. As the United States expanded westward, the existing slave-holding states wanted to expand the laws of slavery to these new states.

Lincoln was against extending slavery to the new states but vowed he would not interfere with slavery in the states in which it already existed. By stopping its expansion, he hoped to curb the power of the slave states, keep the country whole, and eventually bring an end to slavery.

Lincoln was nominated for president in 1860 by the Republicans. He was the moderate choice. In the national election, he faced three opponents, including nominees from the Constitutional Union, Northern Democratic, and Southern Democratic parties. With just 39.8% of the vote, Lincoln won. The second-leading vote getter, with 29.5% of the vote, was Stephen Douglas, the same man who had earlier defeated Lincoln in the Senate race.

"The Very Survival of the United States"

Like Barack Obama, Lincoln had very little government experience when he entered office, but he learned quickly. The man who had "fought only musketoes" was now responsible for the most important war America had fought to date—the Civil War. As historian James McPherson writes: "The very survival of the United States depended on how he performed his duties as commander in chief." Lincoln devoted himself night and day to learning about military matters and within a few years became the best "war president" the country has ever had.

Yet it was more than just as commander in chief that Lincoln excelled. Lincoln—still "on a hunt after an idea"—grew to believe strongly in full freedom for slaves and in the importance of keeping the Union together, no matter what terrible sacrifices needed to be made. And he instilled this idea in the American people through a series of speeches, like the Gettysburg Address and his second inaugural address.

In the spring of 1865, the Civil War was about to end with victory for the North. One likes to think that Abraham Lincoln would then go back to Springfield and practice law, and tell tall stories down at the neighborhood grocery store, as he often said he would. But it was not to be. On April 14, Abraham Lincoln went to see a play at Ford's Theatre in Washington D.C. He was tired, he told his wife Mary, and did not want to go, but "people expected" that he would be there. Waiting for Lincoln in the theater was a Southern sympathizer named John Wilkes Booth, who was enraged that Lincoln had not only freed the slaves, but was now planning on giving them full equality, including the right to vote. While Lincoln sat quietly watching the play, holding Mary's hand, Booth snuck up on him and shot him in the head. Abraham Lincoln died the next morning, April 15, 1865, without ever regaining consciousness.

Hundreds of thousands had died in the fight against slavery, and now Abraham Lincoln had joined them. But, like the soldiers Lincoln praised at Gettysburg, his sacrifice would not be in vain. Because of Abraham Lincoln's extraordinary life there would indeed be "a new birth of freedom" in America, one that lasts until this day. And for many people President Barack Obama symbolizes this very thing.

January 20, 2009: Immediately after Barack Obama takes the oath of office, his wife, Michelle, gets her first kiss from the new president of the United States.

Introducing Barack Obama

THERE ARE SO MANY FIRSTS associated with Barack Obama. He's the first president with a name as distinctive as Barack Obama, the first president born in Hawaii, even the first president to have his own MySpace page! The most important first is that in 220 years of America's existence, he is our first African American president.

Like Abraham Lincoln, Barack Obama had an unusual and in some ways difficult childhood, but it was one that allowed him to develop empathy for those in pain or trouble. He was born on August 4, 1961, in Honolulu, Hawaii. His father, Barack Obama, Sr., was from the African country of Kenya. His mother, Ann Dunham, was from a small town in Kansas. Both of them were studying at the University of Hawaii when they met. Barack Obama, Sr., was the school's first black student. They fell in love, got married, and had a son, whom they named Barack, which means "blessing" in Swahili, a native African language. Obama's middle name, Hussein, comes from his Kenyan grandfather, Hussein Onyango Obama.

When Barack was two, his parents divorced. His father eventually returned to Kenya, and his mother remarried. Barack's stepfather was also a student. He was from Indonesia, in Southeast Asia. Young Barack and his mother moved to Jakarta, the capital of Indonesia, where Barack lived until he was ten. At that time, because his mother was continuing her work in Indonesia and she thought Barack would get a better education in Hawaii, he returned to Honolulu. There he was raised by his grandparents on his mother's side. From fifth through twelfth grade, he attended the Punahou School, a well-known private school.

From Barry to Barack

Barack graduated with honors in 1979, but in some ways his life was a tough one. He admitted to trying drugs and alcohol in high school—a poor choice that represented "the struggles and confusion of a teenage boy," as he later put it. The absence of his father was difficult for him. When he was twelve, his father returned to Hawaii for a month-long visit. After that visit, Barack would never see his father again. His father died in a car accident in Africa in 1982.

Obama would later write, "I was trying to raise myself to be a black man in America, but having a hard time knowing how to do it." This was especially difficult in Hawaii, where the number of African Americans was small. In fact, while he was in high school, Obama told few people that his real first name was Barack. He introduced himself as Barry.

From Hawaii, Obama went to California, where he studied for two years at Occidental College before transferring to Columbia University in New York. After he graduated, he went to Chicago—the city that he would eventually call home—and became a community organizer. He helped poor people to improve their lives by setting up job training programs and by organizing them into groups to fight for their rights. While his friends still called him Barry, he was no longer ashamed of introducing himself as Barack.

After a few years in Chicago, Obama went to Harvard University in Cambridge, Massachusetts, where he studied law and graduated with highest honors. In the summer of 1988, while working part-time in a Chicago law firm, he met his future wife, Michelle Robinson, who had also attended Harvard Law School. She later described him as wearing a "bad sports jacket" and having "a cigarette dangling from his mouth." (Obama has struggled with quitting smoking.) But she found herself liking him because, despite his obvious talent and intelligence, "he didn't take himself too seriously."

The two were married in 1992 and would have two children, Malia, now 10, and Sasha, now 7. In the early 1990s, Barack Obama got involved in politics, working for the Democratic Party in Chicago, and—like Lincoln before him—was elected to the Illinois General Assembly. There he continued to work for poor people by helping to pass laws that provided health insurance for those without it. He also sponsored a law that increased funding for the prevention of AIDS.

Basketball: "A Consuming Passion"

Personally, Barack Obama was known to his friends and family for his quiet sense of humor and his love of basketball. Basketball is more than just a sport for Obama. "I could play basketball with a consuming passion that would always exceed my limited talent," he wrote in his memoir *Dreams from My Father*. "At least on the basketball court I could find a community of sorts, with an inner life all its own," Obama said. "It was there that I would make my closest white friends, on turf where blackness couldn't be a disadvantage."

Obama still loves to play. On his historic election day he organized a pickup game with his old friends. "He really feels the game brings him back to a place where he can be completely himself and he can relax," said his sister, Maya.

"Part of the Larger American Story"

In 2004, Barack Obama came to national attention when he gave an important address at the Democratic Convention. Once every four years, when there is a national election for president, the two major parties, the Republicans and Democrats, hold a convention where they officially nominate their candidate. Obama, then known to few Americans outside his home state of Illinois, was running for the United States Senate.

"Let's face it," he began. "My presence on this stage is pretty unlikely." He introduced himself by describing his mixed heritage and out-of-the-ordinary upbringing. "I stand here today grateful for the diversity of my heritage," he continued. "I stand here knowing that my story is part of the larger American story, that I owe a debt to all those who came before me." By this he meant that those Americans who worked for freedom and equality in the past had made it possible for Barack Obama, born of a white mother and a black father, to run for the United States Senate, one of the highest offices in the land. We live, he said, "in a generous America." He added to thunderous applause, "There's not a liberal America and a conservative America; there's the United States of America."

Obama won his race for senator. One of the key roles of the Senate is to establish laws by sponsoring what are called bills. One bill that Obama sponsored established awards that would help college students pay off their loans. He also worked on the Veterans' Affairs Committee. Obama joined with other senators in trying to improve conditions for soldiers returning from the war in Iraq—a war that Obama opposed.

Then came the longest presidential campaign in American history. In early 2007, more than a year before the election, Hillary Clinton, John Edwards, John McCain, and numerous other politicians all announced that they were running for president. So did Barack Obama, the junior senator from Illinois. After a hard battle, Obama became the Democratic Party nominee.

To the White House: A Legacy for Hope

He then won the 2008 election, beating the Republican John McCain by about 7% of the vote (a margin of about ten million votes). Obama's focus on fixing the problems in our nation's economy helped, as did his desire to end the war in Iraq.

While President Obama is trying to fix the country's problems, his children, Malia and Sasha, will be finding their way around the historic White House. They are the youngest children in the White House since Amy Carter, President Jimmy Carter's daughter, arrived there in 1977 at the age of nine.

The first floor of the mansion is for public viewing, but the first family has the entire second floor to themselves. This area contains sixteen rooms, including five bedrooms, a living room, and a kitchen. First lady (and mother) Michelle says that while there is a staff of eighty to help things run smoothly, both Malia and Sasha will be expected to make their own beds. That's a small price to pay for the kind of fun they're going to have. The White House has a swimming pool, a bowling alley, a small outdoor basketball court, a tennis court, a secret children's garden, and even a chef who will make pizza just for the kids. Helping out will be their grandmother, Marian Robinson, who is moving to the White House to help keep an eye on the girls.

At the end of his book *The Audacity of Hope*, Obama describes how, when he first came to Washington D.C. as a senator, he liked to visit the Lincoln Memorial late at night, when few people were around. He loved the quiet, loved to see the larger-than-life sculpture of Abraham Lincoln looking majestically out over the National Mall, loved to read the words of the Gettysburg Address and the Second Inaugural Address, which are inscribed on the walls there. While he was there, he liked to think about "America, and those who built it," not only the great Abraham Lincoln or Martin Luther King, Jr., but also the "nameless, faceless men and women . . . constructing lives for themselves and their children."

In *The Audacity of Hope*, Obama states that he wants to leave behind "a legacy that will make our children's lives more hopeful than our own." And, as he stood before the nation and was inaugurated as our forty-fourth president, millions of Americans placed their hopes for a better tomorrow with him.

December 4, 1783: George Washington formally bids farewell to his officers in New York before resigning as commander in chief. Six years later, he became the first president of the United States.

6.

United States Presidents: From Washington to Obama

THERE HAVE BEEN fifty-six planned presidential inaugurations, as well as nine unplanned ones when presidents either died or resigned.

Most of the planned inaugural ceremonies begin when the president-elect—the person who is about to become president—picks up the outgoing president at the White House and they ride together to the Capitol Building.

In the nineteenth century, presidents gave their inaugural address before taking their oath of office, but since the beginning of the twentieth century presidents have been sworn in first and then give their speech. Almost always, the chief justice of the Supreme Court swears in the president. The justice slowly and clearly states the thirty-five-word oath of office, and the new president repeats it along with him or occasionally says it after him. The president usually swears his oath on a Bible, but not always, and there is no requirement in the Constitution that says he must do so.

The president then gives his inaugural speech. The length of the speech has ranged from over eight thousand words (William Henry Harrison's) to 135 words (George Washington's second inauguration). These days, a presidential inaugural address usually runs about fifteen hundred to two thousand words and takes about half an hour to deliver.

After that, let the party begin! The new president attends an inaugural luncheon sponsored by Congress and then goes off to watch the colorful inaugural parade with his family and the vice president. That evening, the president and first lady make their appearance at numerous inaugural balls—there are often as many as nine or ten. After dancing and speaking with well-wishers, the president and his family then return to the White House for their first night in the historic mansion.

The next day, with all the festivities over, it's time to get down to business and begin the job of running the country.

President: George Washington

Term of Presidency: 1789–1797
Political Party: Federalist
Inauguration Dates: April 30, 1789; March 4, 1793
Inaugural Facts & Firsts:

George Washington took the oath of office at Federal Hall in New York. He was sworn in by New York State Chancellor Robert Livingston on a balcony overlooking a cheering crowd. Then he went inside and gave his inaugural address to Congress. George Washington was the very first president to be inaugurated, and the first to utter the words "So help me God!" after the oath, a precedent most presidents follow. He then kissed the Bible he had rested his hand on. Four future presidents would use this same Bible at their swearing-in ceremonies (Warren G. Harding, Dwight Eisenhower, Jimmy Carter, and George H. W. Bush). At other times, the Bible is kept in the National Archives in Washington. George Washington's second inaugural address was the shortest ever given—135 words.

President: John Adams

Term of Presidency: 1797–1801
Political Party: Federalist
Inauguration Date: March 4, 1797

Inaugural Facts & Firsts:
John Adams's inauguration took place in Philadelphia, where Congress was temporarily housed. Congress and the president later moved to the new capital city of Washington. The sharp-tongued Adams was a little jealous of the response to the departure of President George Washington. Adams wrote his wife, Abigail, about "the tears, the full eyes, the streaming eyes, the trickling eyes." Adams was the first president to receive the oath of office from the chief justice of the United States. This practice is always followed now unless there are unexpected circumstances, like the death or resignation of a president.

President: Thomas Jefferson
Term of Presidency: 1801–1809
Political Party: Republican
Inauguration Dates: March 4, 1801; March 4, 1805
Inaugural Facts & Firsts:
Thomas Jefferson was the first president to make a famous statement in his inaugural address, saying: "We are all Federalists, we are all Republicans," meaning that we are Americans first. This is a theme echoed by presidents all the way down the line to Barack Obama. Jefferson was the first president to be inaugurated in Washington D.C. He was the first

and probably the only president to walk both to and from his inauguration. His inauguration also featured the first informal parade down Pennsylvania Avenue. The outgoing president, John Adams, became the first president to refuse to attend his successor's inauguration.

President: James Madison

Term of Presidency: 1809–1817
Political Party: Republican
Inauguration Dates: March 4, 1809; March 4, 1813
Inaugural Facts & Firsts:
James Madison's first inauguration featured the very first official inaugural parade and the very first inaugural ball to be held on the day of the inauguration itself. That day, he also became the first president to wear inaugural-day clothing made entirely in the United States. His jacket was from Hartford, Connecticut, and his breeches, stockings, and shoes were from New York. Madison's second inauguration, during the War of 1812 against the British, became the first inauguration to be held during wartime.

President: James Monroe

Term of Presidency: 1817–1825
Political Party: Republican

Inauguration Dates: March 4, 1817; March 5, 1821
Inaugural Facts & Firsts:
James Monroe's first inauguration was the first to be held entirely outdoors, both the oath-taking and the inaugural address. It was a good thing the weather was warm and sunny. Monroe set a precedent by delaying his second inauguration to Monday because it fell on a Sunday. His second inauguration featured the very first appearance of the United States Marine Band at an inauguration. It played "Hail, Columbia," a song that was originally composed for George Washington's inauguration. It was considered the unofficial national anthem of the United States until it was replaced by "The Star-Spangled Banner" in 1931.

President: John Quincy Adams
Term of Presidency: 1825–1829
Political Party: National-Republican
Inauguration Date: March 4, 1825
Inaugural Facts & Firsts:
John Quincy Adams became the first son of a president to become president himself. He was also the first president to wear long pants during the swearing-in ceremonies (the others had worn breeches, or knickers). Almost every president has used a Bible to be

sworn in, but John Quincy Adams used a book on constitutional law instead. Like his father, Adams chose not to attend his successor's inauguration.

President: Andrew Jackson

Term of Presidency: 1829–1837
Political Party: Democratic-Republican
Inauguration Dates: March 4, 1829; March 4, 1833
Inaugural Facts & Firsts:
Andrew Jackson's first inauguration was the first held at the East Portico of the Capitol Building. Thereafter, most inaugurations were held there until they were switched to the West Front of the Capitol Building in 1981. Jackson's first inauguration also featured the wildest inauguration party in the history of Washington. Crowds of people swarmed the White House, destroying furniture and delicate china dishes, and forcing the new president to seek shelter elsewhere in order to get some rest.

President: Martin Van Buren

Term of Presidency: 1837–1841
Political Party: Democratic
Inauguration Date: March 4, 1837
Inaugural Facts & Firsts:

Martin Van Buren was the first person born a United States citizen to be sworn into the presidency. He also set a precedent as being the first person to call on the previous president (in this case, Andrew Jackson) at the White House and ride with him to the Capitol Building for the swearing-in, a procedure that is now always followed. Van Buren's inauguration also featured the first inaugural programs, the first floats in the inaugural parade, and the first time two balls were held on inauguration day.

President: William Henry Harrison

Term of Presidency: 1841
Political Party: Whig
Inauguration Date: March 4, 1841
Inaugural Facts & Firsts:
William Henry Harrison became the first president to arrive in Washington by train for the inauguration. He gave the longest inaugural address in presidential history (more than eight thousand words) while standing outdoors on a freezing cold day without wearing a coat or hat. He did this to show how fit he was because, at age sixty-eight, he was the oldest man, up to that point, to take the oath of office. Unfortunately, after standing for an hour and forty

minutes in the wind and cold, he came down with pneumonia. He died a month later, the first president to die in office.

President: John Tyler

Term of Presidency: 1841–1845
Political Party: Whig
Inauguration Date: April 6, 1841
Inaugural Facts & Firsts:
Because of the death of President William Henry Harrison, John Tyler became the first vice president to take office after the death of a president. He was sworn in at his residence in Washington, Brown's Indian Queen Hotel, by William Cranch, chief justice of the U.S. District Court in Washington (the chief justice of the Supreme Court was out of town). Just before he was inaugurated, he told his children: "My children, by a deplored event, I am unexpectedly elevated to the presidency of the United States. You, as my children, will rise with me. I beg you ever to bear in mind that this promotion is only temporary." By his two wives, Tyler had more children than any other president in American history—fifteen all together.

President: James Polk

Term of Presidency: 1845–1849
Political Party: Democratic
Inauguration Date: March 4, 1845
Inaugural Facts & Firsts:
Polk, at forty-nine, was the youngest man up to that time to take the oath of office. He traveled from his home in Tennessee by steamer, carriage, and train to get to Washington. He gave his inaugural address in a cold, driving rain, facing a sea of umbrellas. His inaugural address was the first to be transmitted by telegraph. The Marine Band played "Hail to the Chief" for the first time after he took the oath of office. This song is now always used to introduce the president.

President: Zachary Taylor

Term of Presidency: 1849–1850
Political Party: Whig
Inauguration Date: March 5, 1849
Inaugural Facts & Firsts:
Zachary Taylor was the second president whose inauguration day fell on a Sunday, so out of respect for the Sabbath he too postponed his swearing-in until Monday, March 5. Thirty thousand people braved very

cold weather to show up for his inauguration. Fortunately, considering the extreme weather, he kept his remarks relatively brief. Reporters praised his speech, although they said that he was, in person, "somewhat stouter" than they had expected.

President: Millard Fillmore

Term of Presidency: 1850–1853
Political Party: Whig
Inauguration Date: July 10, 1850
Inaugural Facts & Firsts:
After Zachary Taylor died of illness on July 9, 1850, Millard Fillmore became the second vice president to take over in office. He was given the oath at a special meeting of the House of Representatives and the Senate by William Cranch, the same justice who had given John Tyler his oath. Fillmore did not make an inaugural address, but did send a message to Congress a few days later talking about his grief for the "great man" who "has fallen among us."

President: Franklin Pierce

Term of Presidency: 1853–1857
Political Party: Democratic
Inauguration Date: March 4, 1853

Inaugural Facts & Firsts:
A terrible accident happened to president-elect Franklin Pierce and his family on their way to Washington D.C. for his inauguration. Their train crashed and Pierce's eleven-year-old son, Benjamin, was killed before his parents' eyes. He was their third son to die of either accident or illness. Pierce thought he was being punished by God because his faith was not strong enough. When he took the oath of office, he became the first and thus far the only president to affirm and not to "swear" his oath (this is allowed by the Constitution). By affirming the oath, he was simply repeating and agreeing to the oath, not swearing to God to uphold it. Franklin Pierce delivered his entire inaugural address from memory. He was the first president to do so.

President: James Buchanan
Term of Presidency: 1857–1861
Political Party: Democratic
Inauguration Date: March 4, 1857
Inaugural Facts & Firsts:
James Buchanan's inauguration is the first for which a photo exists. If Buchanan looked a little uncomfortable as he gave his speech it was because he had

a bad case of diarrhea and hadn't been able to eat solid food for several days. His doctor came with him to the inauguration and stood nearby as he gave his address and took the oath. Buchanan was able to finish the ceremony without difficulty and even attend his inaugural parade. One of the floats in the parade was built to look just like the famous ship *USS Constitution* ("Old Ironsides"), which fought in the war of 1812 and was a symbol of American patriotism. Buchanan was also able to make an appearance at his inaugural ball, where, for the first time, gas light, instead of candles, was used at an inaugural event.

President: Abraham Lincoln

Term of Presidency: 1861–1865
Political Party: Republican
Inauguration Dates: March 4, 1861; March 4, 1865
Inaugural Facts & Firsts:

Abraham Lincoln's first inauguration is known for the large amount of police and military protection surrounding the president-elect. This was because Lincoln had received so many threats from those in the South who did not like his policy against slavery. At his first inaugural ball, Lincoln shook hands with the public for over two hours. Lincoln's second inauguration was the first one in which African Americans—Union soldiers—marched in an inaugural parade. His second inaugural address, considered one of the most famous speeches in American history, is now inscribed on the Lincoln Memorial. Although today vice presidents no longer give their own inaugural speeches, this was common practice at the time of Lincoln's inauguration. But Vice President Andrew Johnson was drunk, and Lincoln told a guard: "Do not let Johnson speak outside."

President: Andrew Johnson

Term of Presidency: 1865–1869

Political Party: Republican

Inauguration Date: April 15, 1865

Inaugural Facts & Firsts:

After Lincoln became the first president ever to be assassinated, his vice president, Andrew Johnson, was sworn in as president by Chief Justice of the Supreme Court Salmon P. Chase. This was the first time a Supreme Court justice administered the oath to the vice president after the president's death. Johnson made a short speech after he was sworn in. He was not drunk this time, but the speech disappointed those who heard it, since he barely mentioned the dead president and spoke mainly about his own troubles ("My life, as a public servant, has been a laborious one"). Disliked and nearly thrown out of office by his political opponents, Johnson refused to attend the inauguration of his successor, Ulysses S. Grant.

President: Ulysses S. Grant

Term of Presidency: 1869–1877
Political Party: Republican
Inauguration Dates: March 4, 1869; March 4, 1873
Inaugural Facts & Firsts:
Civil War hero Grant's first inauguration marked the first time that the governors of states were officially invited to the inauguration. This practice has been followed ever since. It was 16 degrees during Grant's second inauguration, the second coldest inauguration day ever (Ronald Reagan's second inauguration was the coldest). The wind blew so hard during Grant's address that his speech was nearly torn out of his hands and most people in the audience could barely hear him. At the parade it was so cold that drummer boys cried—and the tears froze to their cheeks. The food at Grant's inaugural ball was frozen. Canaries brought in to sing to the guests froze in their cages while the few guests who showed up danced in their overcoats.

President: Rutherford B. Hayes
Term of Presidency: 1877–1881
Political Party: Republican
Inauguration Dates: March 3, 1877; March 5, 1877
Inaugural Facts & Firsts:
The election of Rutherford B. Hayes was one of the most controversial presidential elections in U.S. history. Many people felt that the Republican Party stole their victory from the Democrats and their candidate, Samuel Tilden. Because March 4 in 1877 fell on a Sunday, the inaugural ceremony was planned for Monday, as had been the case with James Monroe and Zachary Taylor. However, the outgoing president, Ulysses S. Grant, was so concerned that there might be rioting or unrest in the country that he had Hayes secretly sworn in at the White House on the evening of Saturday, March 3. (Hayes refused to take his oath on the Sabbath because he was very religious.) Hayes was then sworn in publicly on Monday, March 5. For the first and only time, the United States had two presidents for one day in history, March 4.

President: James Garfield
Term of Presidency: 1881
Political Party: Republican

Inauguration Date: March 4, 1881
Inaugural Facts & Firsts:
James Garfield's inauguration marked two firsts: It was the first time the mother of a president (Eliza Garfield) attended her son's inauguration, and it was also the first time the president reviewed the inaugural parade from a stand in front of the White House. This is a practice that is now always followed. Garfield's inauguration was also the first time that a woman—actually women: Garfield's wife, Lucy, as well as his mother—were allowed to sit in the front row at the swearing-in. Previously, women sat in the very last row of seats on the inaugural platform, no matter what their relation to the president.

President: Chester Arthur
Term of Presidency: 1881–1885
Political Party: Republican
Inauguration Date: September 20, 1881
Inaugural Facts & Firsts:
On July 2, 1881, James Garfield was shot and seriously wounded by a crazed man who was unhappy that Garfield did not give him a job. Two and a half months later, on September 19, Garfield died, becoming the second president in United States history to

be assassinated. His vice president, Chester Arthur, was sworn in as president at his home in New York, at 1:30 in the morning of September 20. Two days later, on September 22, he took the oath of office again in a small ceremony in the vice president's room at the Capitol Building. Two ex-presidents—Ulysses S. Grant and Rutherford B. Hayes—were present. Arthur made a brief statement, saying: "Though the chosen of the people be struck down, his constitutional successor is peacefully installed without shock or strain."

President: Grover Cleveland

Term of Presidency: 1885–1889; 1893–1897
Political Party: Democratic
Inauguration Dates: March 4, 1885; March 4, 1893
Inaugural Facts & Firsts:
One of the few Democrats to be elected to the presidency in the nineteenth century, Grover Cleveland—who was nicknamed "Grover the Good" because of his honesty—was also the first president to be elected to two nonconsecutive terms. He became president in 1885, lost to Benjamin Harrison in 1888, and then became president again in 1893. Grover Cleveland, like Franklin Pierce, memorized his entire

first and second inaugural addresses. At Cleveland's first inauguration, electric lights lit up an inaugural ball for the first time. At his second swearing-in ceremony, the weather was so cold (25 degrees) that when Grover Cleveland took off his top hat to make his speech, the crowd yelled: "Put on your hat!" They were afraid he would catch cold. But Cleveland delivered his speech bare-headed anyway.

President: Benjamin Harrison

Term of Presidency: 1889–1893

Political Party: Republican

Inauguration Date: March 4, 1889

Inaugural Facts & Firsts:

Often called the president who came *in between* Grover Cleveland, Harrison made an undistinguished inaugural address in rainy and windy weather. The ceremony was marked by the courtesy of outgoing president Grover Cleveland, who held an umbrella over Harrison's head while the new president gave his speech. After the inaugural ceremony, the former first lady, Frances Cleveland, told one of the White House servants to take good care of everything. Why? he asked her. "Because we are coming back just four years from today," Frances Cleveland told him. And she was right.

President: William McKinley

Term of Presidency: 1897–1901
Political Party: Republican
Inauguration Dates: March 4, 1897; March 4, 1901
Inaugural Facts & Firsts:
William McKinley's first inauguration was the first to be recorded by motion picture cameras. McKinley was the first president to have a glass-enclosed viewing stand in front of the White House. His second inauguration marked the first time that the House of Representatives joined the Senate in making plans for the swearing-in of the president. This was the start of the Joint Congressional Committee on Inauguration Ceremonies (JCCIC).

President: Theodore Roosevelt

Term of Presidency: 1901–1909
Political Party: Republican
Inauguration Dates: September 14, 1901; March 4, 1905
Inaugural Facts & Firsts:
William McKinley was shot in Buffalo, New York, on September 6, 1901. He died on September 14, becoming the third American president to be assassinated in thirty-six years. His vice president, Theodore Roosevelt, who was vacationing in the Adirondack

Mountains of New York, hastily returned to Buffalo and was sworn in at a friend's home by U.S. Federal District Judge John R. Hazel on September 14. At age forty-two, he became America's youngest president ever (although John F. Kennedy, age forty-three when sworn in, became the country's youngest *elected* president). In 1904, Roosevelt then became the first vice president who took over from a president who died in office to be elected to another term of office on his own. At his inauguration in 1905, telephones were installed on the Capitol grounds for the very first time.

President: William H. Taft

Term of Presidency: 1909–1913
Political Party: Republican
Inauguration Date: March 4, 1909
Inaugural Facts & Firsts:
The inauguration of William H. Taft—who had been Theodore Roosevelt's vice president—was marked by such a heavy blizzard (ten inches of snow) that the swearing-in ceremony had to be moved indoors. Taft joked: "I always knew it would be a cold day when I became president." Still, his inauguration marked a couple of firsts. It was the first time a president's

wife would ride with him in the procession from the Capitol Building to the White House. It was also the first time an automobile made its appearance in an inaugural parade, although the president was not in it at the time.

President: Woodrow Wilson

Term of Presidency: 1913–1921
Political Party: Democratic
Inauguration Dates: March 4, 1913; March 4, 1917
Inaugural Facts & Firsts:
Wilson's wife, Ellen, rode to the Capitol with him for the oath-taking, the first time this had ever happened. Wilson did not hold an inaugural ball for either of his inaugurations. He thought an inauguration was too serious an occasion for dancing. "It will be most pleasing to me," Wilson said, "to be simply sworn in . . . and turn at once to the work which will be calling." (There would be no further inaugural balls until 1933.) Wilson's second inauguration fell on a Sunday, and he became the first president to allow himself to be sworn in that day, although the official ceremony was held the next day. For the first time, women marched in the inaugural parade.

President: Warren G. Harding
Term of Presidency: 1921–1923
Political Party: Republican
Inauguration Date: March 4, 1921
Inaugural Facts & Firsts:
After winning the first presidential election in which women could vote nationwide, Harding became the first president to ride to and from his inauguration in a car. During his oath of office and speech, loudspeakers were used for the first time to amplify his words for the audience. He was sworn in using the same Bible as George Washington had used in the first U.S. presidential inauguration.

President: Calvin Coolidge
Term of Presidency: 1923–1929
Political Party: Republican
Inauguration Dates: August 3, 1923; March 4, 1925
Inaugural Facts & Firsts:
President Harding died of a heart attack on August 2, 1923, while in a San Francisco hotel. His vice president, Calvin Coolidge, was vacationing at the time at his father's home in a tiny village in Vermont. It did not have a telephone or electricity. When Coolidge finally received word that Hard-

ing had died, he took the oath of office from his father (who was a justice of the peace, and used to performing minor ceremonies). This is the first and only time a father has ever given the presidential oath of office to his son. Because officials in Washington were not sure a justice of the peace could actually perform the ceremony, they made Coolidge retake the oath on August 17. Coolidge's second inauguration in 1925 marked the first time that a presidential inauguration was broadcast nationally on radio, as well as the first time an ex-president, William H. Taft, gave the oath of office, as Supreme Court chief justice.

President: Herbert Hoover

Term of Presidency: 1929–1933

Political Party: Republican

Inauguration Date: March 4, 1929

Inaugural Facts & Firsts:

This was the first inauguration to be recorded by a sound newsreel, which people could watch in movie theaters. This is important because somehow a rumor began after the ceremony that Hoover had "affirmed" his oath, as Franklin Pierce did. Hoover's Quaker religion did not approve of swearing oaths. But according to inaugural historian Jim Bendat, the newsreel shows that the phrase "solemnly swear" was part of the oath—and Hoover replied: "I do."

President: Franklin D. Roosevelt

Term of Presidency: 1933–1945
Political Party: Democratic
Inauguration Dates: March 4, 1933; January 20, 1937; January 20, 1941; January 20, 1945
Inaugural Facts & Firsts:

Franklin Roosevelt had more inauguration ceremonies than any U.S. president has ever had, or ever will. He was elected president four times but now, because of the Twenty-second Amendment to the Constitution, a person can serve no more than two terms as president. At his first inauguration in 1933, as the financial problems of the Great Depression were just beginning, he gave his famous speech in which he told Americans that "the only thing we have to fear is fear itself." His second inauguration became the first ever to take place on January 20. The date of the turnover of power was moved up from March 4 to January 20 by the Twentieth Amendment to the Constitution.

President: Harry S. Truman

Term of Presidency: 1945–1953
Political Party: Democratic
Inauguration Dates: April 12, 1945; January 20, 1949
Inaugural Facts & Firsts:

When President Franklin Roosevelt died of a stroke on April 12, 1945, at his vacation home in Warm Springs, Georgia, Vice President Harry Truman was left with big shoes to fill. Roosevelt had led the country through the Depression and almost four years of world war. When Truman first heard the news of Roosevelt's death, he exclaimed: "Jesus Christ and General Jackson!" After taking the oath of office in the White House Cabinet Room, he said to reporters: "Boys, if you ever pray, pray for me now." Truman's second inauguration in 1949 was the first ever to be televised.

President: Dwight D. Eisenhower

Term of Presidency: 1953–1961
Political Party: Republican
Inauguration Dates: January 20, 1953; January 21, 1957
Inaugural Facts & Firsts:

Former general Dwight Eisenhower used two Bibles when he took his oath of office at his first inaugural in 1953—the one used by George Washington in 1789, as well as one Eisenhower's mother gave him when he graduated from West Point. Eisenhower broke with tradition by wearing a homburg hat (a stiff hat made of wool or fur felt with a dent running down the center and a curled-up brim) instead of the traditional stovepipe or top hat. Eisenhower's second inauguration in 1957 fell on a Sunday, so he was sworn in privately that day and had his public ceremony on Monday, January 21.

President: John F. Kennedy

Term of Presidency: 1961–1963
Political Party: Democratic
Inauguration Date: January 20, 1961
Inaugural Facts & Firsts:

John F. Kennedy became the first Catholic to be sworn in as president and also, at age forty-three, the youngest person to be elected president. For the first time a poet, Robert Frost, would be a part of the inauguration ceremonies. Poets have now read their work at four inaugurations—Robert Frost in 1961, Maya Angelou in 1993, Miller Williams in 1997, and Elizabeth Alexander in 2009. Kennedy's inauguration speech contained the famous line "Ask not what your country can do for you; ask what you can do for your country." Kennedy's was the first inauguration to be televised in color and the first to be celebrated with five inaugural balls. Flamethrowers were used for the first and last time to clear snow off of Pennsylvania Avenue for the inaugural parade. Kennedy was the last president to wear a top hat to his inauguration.

President: Lyndon B. Johnson

Term of Presidency: 1963–1969

Political Party: Democratic

Inauguration Dates: November 22, 1963; January 20, 1965

Inaugural Facts & Firsts:

Shortly after President Kennedy was killed in Dallas, Texas, on November 22, 1963, becoming the fourth U.S. president to die by an assassin's bullet, his vice president, Lyndon Johnson, was sworn in as president on Air Force One at Dallas's Love Field. He became the first president to be sworn in by a woman—U.S. District Judge Sarah T. Hughes. At Johnson's inauguration after being reelected in 1964, his wife, Lady Bird Johnson, became the first first lady to take part in the swearing-in, by holding the Bible for her husband. This was also the first time that a limousine with bullet proof glass enclosing the president was used in an inaugural procession.

President: Richard Nixon

Term of Presidency: 1969–1974

Political Party: Republican

Inauguration Dates: January 20, 1969; January 20, 1973

Inaugural Facts & Firsts:

Richard Nixon's inauguration became the first to be disrupted by protestors—in this case, people protesting against the Vietnam War. Nixon was protected by about nine thousand police, army troops, and National Guardsmen. Because Nixon had been Dwight Eisenhower's vice president for eight years, he had attended numerous inauguration balls, but he didn't dance at one until his second inauguration in 1973, where he did the fox-trot with his wife, Pat.

President: Gerald R. Ford

Term of Presidency: 1974–1977

Political Party: Republican

Inauguration Date: August 9, 1974

Inaugural Facts & Firsts:

When President Nixon resigned after being threatened with impeachment, Vice President Gerald Ford took the oath of office in the White House from Chief Justice Warren Burger. In a short address, he said: "My fellow Americans, our long national nightmare is over." Since Ford had been appointed vice president when Nixon's previously elected vice president, Spiro Agnew, resigned after being charged with a crime, Ford became the first unelected vice president to become president. He was also the first vice president to become chief executive after the resignation of a president.

President: Jimmy Carter

Term of Presidency: 1977–1981

Political Party: Democratic

Inauguration Date: January 20, 1977

Inaugural Facts & Firsts:

James Earl Carter took the oath of office as "Jimmy" Carter, therefore becoming the first president to be sworn in using a nickname. He used both George Washington's Bible and an old family Bible. He became the first president to walk all the way from the Capitol to the White House after taking his oath of office. His inauguration was the first time solar heat was used to keep the president and others warm in the reviewing stand, and also the first time there was access for the handicapped to watch the parade.

President: Ronald Reagan
Term of Presidency: 1981–1989
Political Party: Republican
Inauguration Dates: January 20, 1981; January 21, 1985
Inaugural Facts & Firsts:
At the age of sixty-nine in 1981, Ronald Reagan became the oldest person inaugurated president—a record he held until he was reelected and inaugurated again, on January 21, 1985. His was the first inauguration to be held on the West Front of the Capitol Building, a practice presidents have followed ever since. Nine inaugural balls were held after Reagan's first inauguration—the most ever up to that point—and they were transmitted by satellite to thirty-two other ballrooms around the country. Reagan's second inauguration fell on a Sunday, so he was sworn in privately that day and had his official swearing in on January 21, 1985. However, this was the coldest inauguration day on record, with a wind chill factor of up to 20 degrees below zero, so the swearing-in was held inside the Capitol Building.

President: George H. W. Bush
Term of Presidency: 1989–1993
Political Party: Republican
Inauguration Date: January 20, 1989
Inaugural Facts & Firsts:
To commemorate the two hundredth anniversary of the presidency, George H. W. Bush became the fifth president to take the oath of office on the same Bible as George Washington in 1789. In his inaugural address, George Bush, who had been Ronald Reagan's vice president, called presidential inaugurations "Democracy's big day." His diary of the day read: "6 a.m.—catch 3 news shows. Drink coffee—Play with grand kids—Pray—Go to WHouse—Get Sworn in."

President: William J. Clinton
Term of Presidency: 1993–2001
Political Party: Democratic
Inauguration Dates: January 20, 1993; January 20, 1997
Inaugural Facts & Firsts:
Most presidents now hug their wives after being sworn-in, but President Bill Clinton was so happy he hugged everyone around him, except for Chief Justice William Rehnquist, who had given him the oath of

office. Clinton's 1997 inauguration was the first to be broadcast live on the internet, and also featured a record number of inaugural balls—fourteen in all. It was also the first inauguration that fell on Martin Luther King Jr. Day, which became an official federal holiday in 1983.

President: George W. Bush

Term of Presidency: 2001–2009
Political Party: Republican
Inauguration Dates: January 20, 2001; January 20, 2005
Inaugural Facts & Firsts:
George W. Bush's first inauguration marked the two hundredth anniversary of the first inauguration to be held in Washington D.C., Thomas Jefferson's. Former President George H. W. Bush became the first president to personally witness the inauguration of his son, George W. Bush. George W. Bush's election to the presidency had been very close. Due to legal challenges regarding counting votes, the final result was not made official until January 5, just fifteen days before the inauguration. There were numerous protestors at his inauguration, and a then-record number of police officers and army troops patrolled Washington.

President: Barack Obama

Term of Presidency: 2009–
Political Party: Democratic
Inauguration Date: January 20, 2009
Inaugural Facts & Firsts:

Barack Obama is the first African American to become president of the United States and the first president since John F. Kennedy to move directly from the Senate to the White House. Over one million people attended his swearing-in ceremony, making it the largest crowd in inaugural history. He recited the oath using the same Bible that Abraham Lincoln used at his first inauguration. Chief Justice John G. Roberts, Jr., provided a classic oath-taking flub—instead of saying "I will faithfully execute the office of president of the United States," he put "faithfully" at the end, confusing President Obama momentarily before the men got back on track. The following day, Roberts swore in Obama again--a do-over. White House Counsel Greg Craig said, "We believe that the oath of office was administered effectively and that the president was sworn in appropriately yesterday. But the oath appears in the Constitution itself. And out of an abundance of caution, because there was one word out of sequence, Chief Justice Roberts administered the oath a second time."

Notes

Inaugurations, Past and Present

1. "Our American Revolution . . ." Dr. Donald R. Kennon, interview, Foreign Press Center Briefing, Washington D.C., January 13, 2006. http://fpc.state.gov/fpc/40871.htm.
2. "Here comes my friend . . ." Jim Bendat, *Democracy's Big Day: The Inaugurations of Our President, 1789–2009* (New York: iUniverse Star, 2008), 131.
3. "The most damnable outrage . . ." Gardiner Harris, "The Underside of the Welcome Mat," *New York Times*, November 8, 2008.
4. "On trying days, the portrait . . ." Barack Obama, "What I See in Lincoln's Eyes," *Time*, June 26, 2005.
5. "Overcome personal loss . . ." Ibid.
6. "In the shadow . . ." Rick Pearson and Ray Long, "Obama: I'm Running for President," *Chicago Tribune*, February 10, 2007.
7. "A bit like a basketball player . . ." John F. Harris & Alexander Burns, "Straw Man? Historians Say Obama Is No Lincoln," Politico.com, December 15, 2008.
8. "I'm LeBron, baby . . ." Ibid.
9. "When an election . . ." Bendat, *Democracy's Big Day*, xviii.

10. "Welcome, mighty chief! . . ." Joseph Cummins, *Anything for a Vote: Dirty Tricks, Cheap Shots and October Surprises in U.S. Presidential Elections* (Philadelphia, PA: Quirk Books, 2007), 10.
11. "I would much rather . . ." Smithsonian Books, Eds., *Every Four Years: The American Presidency, Revised Edition* (New York: W.W. Norton, 1984), 143.
12. "Some ladies displayed . . ." Paul F. Boller, Jr., *Presidential Inaugurations* (New York: Harcourt, Inc., 2001), 203.
13. "Spinach! The two of us . . ." Ibid, 96.
14. "The most history-laden . . ." Ibid, 175.

"A New Birth of Freedom": Setting the Scene

15. "Short, short, short . . . written but not finished." Gettysburg National Military Park, "Lincoln and Gettysburg," essay, http://www.pueblo.gsa.gov/cic_text/misc/gettysburg/g2.htm.
16. "A kind of docudrama . . ." Gary Wills, *Lincoln at Gettysburg: The Words That Remade America* (New York: Simon & Schuster, 1992), 143.
17. "The dedicatory remarks . . ." Herbert Victor Prochnow, *Great Stories from Great Lives* (New York: Harper & Brothers, 1944), 16.

18. "I should be glad, if . . ." American Treasures of the Library of Congress, collection, http://www.loc.gov/exhibits/treasures/trt032.html.

"That Great Gift of Freedom": Setting the Scene

19. "Just pinch me . . ." Ashley Southall, "An Inaugural Dream? 'Pinch Me,' She Says," *New York Times*, January 19, 2009.
20. "A long laundry list . . ." Mary Jo Patterson, "Troubled Boys Step Up to Inaugural Challenge," *New York Times*, January 18, 2009.
21. "I'm not sure whether . . ." Carol Budoff Brown, "A Peek at Obama's Inaugural Plan," Politico.com, December 18, 2008.
22. "First African American president . . ." Mary Ann Akers, "Malia Obama to Dad: Speech 'Better Be Good,'" *Washington Post*, January 15, 2009.
23. "Havin' some fun . . ." Ibid.
24. "You have on the one hand . . ." Benjamin Alexander-Bloch and Jenny Hurwitz, "Inauguration Gives New Resonance to Martin Luther King Jr. Day," *New Orleans Times-Picayune*, January 19, 2009.
25. "Everyone's got to be . . ." Will Higgins, "Obama Leads Day of Service," *Indianapolis Star*, January 20, 2009.

26. "You guys are . . ." Patrick Huguenin, "Next First Lady Michelle Obama a Big Hit at Kids Concert," *New York Daily News*, January 20, 2009.

"We Are Not Enemies, But Friends": Setting the Scene

27. "I have got 4 . . ." Abraham Lincoln Online: Speeches and Writing, http://showcase.netins.net/web/creative/lincoln/speeches/gracebedell.htm.
28. "Dusty and neglected . . ." Stefan Lorant, *The Glorious Burden: The History of the Presidency and Presidential Elections from George Washington to Jimmy Carter* (Lenox, MA: Authors Edition, Inc, 1976), 253.
29. "Lincoln will never . . ." Ibid, 254.
30. "He was tall . . ." Joshua Wolf Shenk, *Lincoln's Melancholy: How Depression Challenged a President and Fueled His Greatness* (Boston: Houghton-Mifflin Company, 2005), 173.
31. "Mediocre presidents run . . ." Ibid, 171.
32. "High-pitched, but resonant . . ." Ibid, 173.
33. "Shall it be peace . . ." "The Speech: An Expert's Guide," William Safire, Newyorktimes.com, January 15, 2009.
34. "Some final words of affection . . ." Davis New-

ton Lott, *The Inaugural Addresses of the American Presidents: From Washington to Kennedy* (New York: Holt, Rinehart & Winston, 1961), 117.

35. "Trembled uncontrollably . . ." Lorant, *The Glorious Burden*, 256.

"With Malice Toward None, with Charity for All": Setting the Scene

36. "Lots of wisdom . . ." Boller, *Presidential Inaugurations*, 154.
37. "With almost a metallic . . ." Herbert Mitgang, *The Fiery Trial: A Life of Lincoln* (New York: Viking Press, 1974), 90.
38. "A profound silence . . ." Boller, *Presidential Inaugurations*, 158.
39. "Did you notice . . ." Mitgang, *The Fiery Trial: A Life of Lincoln*, 92.

Introducing Abraham Lincoln

40. "All in his legs . . ." Stephen B. Oates, *Abraham Lincoln: The Man Behind the Myths* (New York: NAL, 1984), 34.
41. "Was hidden and liked . . ." Shenk, *Lincoln's Melancholy*, 216.
42. "I remember how . . . until I had caught it." James

M. McPherson, *Tried by War: Abraham Lincoln as Commander in Chief* (New York: The Penguin Press, 2008), 2.

43. "The best boy that ever . . ." Mitgang, *The Fiery Trial: A Life of Lincoln*, 14.
44. "A good many struggles . . ." McPherson, *Tried by War*, 1.
45. "If I had another . . ." Harold Holzer, "If I Had Another Face, Do You Think I'd Wear This One?" *American Heritage*, February/March 1983.
46. "The very survival . . ." McPherson, *Tried by War*, 8.

Introducing Barack Obama

47. "The struggles and confusion . . ." Katharine Q. Seelye, "Barack Obama, Asked About Drug History, Admits He Inhaled," *International Herald Tribune*, October 25, 2006.
48. "I was trying . . ." Barack Obama, *The Audacity of Hope: Thoughts on Reclaiming the American Dream* (New York: Three Rivers Press, 2006), 76.
49. "Bad sports jacket . . . dangling from his mouth." David Bergen Brophy, *Michelle Obama: Meet the First Lady* (New York: HarperCollins 2009), 44.
50. "He didn't take himself . . ." Ibid, 45.
51. "At least on . . . be a disadvantage . . ." Jaymes

Song, "Obama Finds Refuge, Identity in Basketball," *USA Today*, June 16, 2008.

52. "He really feels . . ." Ibid.
53. "I stand here today . . ." "Transcript: Illinois Senate Candidate Barack Obama," Washingtonpost.com, July 27, 2004.

United States Presidents: From Washington to Obama

54. "The tears, the full eyes . . ." Boller, *Presidential Inaugurations*, 219.
55. "Somewhat stouter . . ." Ibid, 224.
56. "Great man . . . fallen among us . . ." Ibid, 115.
57. "Though the chosen of . . ." Ibid, 117.
58. "Because we are . . ." Ibid, 228.
59. "I always knew . . ." Ibid, 71.
60. "It will be . . ." Bendat, *Democracy's Big Day*, 136.
61. "Boys, if you ever . . ." Cormac O'Brien, *Secret Lives of U.S. Presidents: What Your Teachers Never Told You About the Men of the White House* (Philadelphia, PA: Quirk Books, 2004), 191.
62. "6 a.m.—catch 3 news shows . . ." Bendat, *Democracy's Big Day*, 4.

Suggested Reading

Bendat, Jim. *Democracy's Big Day: The Inaugurations of Our President, 1789–2009*. New York: iUniverse Star, 2008.

Boller, Paul F., Jr. *Presidential Inaugurations*. New York: Harcourt, Inc., 2001.

Brophy, David Bergen. *Michelle Obama: Meet the First Lady*. New York: Collins/HarperCollins, 2009.

Cummins, Joseph. *Anything for a Vote: Dirty Tricks, Cheap Shots and October Surprises in U.S. Presidential Elections*. Philadelphia, PA: Quirk Books, 2007.

Davis, Kenneth C. and Pedro Martin. *Don't Know Much About the Presidents*. New York: HarperCollins, 2009 (revised edition).

Lorant, Stefan. *The Glorious Burden: The History of the Presidency and Presidential Elections from George Washington to Jimmy Carter*. Lenox, MA: Authors Edition, Inc, 1976.

Lott, Davis Newton. *The Inaugural Addresses of the American Presidents: From Washington to Kennedy*. New York: Holt, Rinehart & Winston, 1961.

McPherson, James M. *Tried by War: Abraham Lincoln as Commander in Chief*. New York: The Penguin Press, 2008.

Mendell, David. *Obama: A Promise of Change*. New York: Amistad/HarperCollins, 2008.

Mitgang, Herbert. *The Fiery Trial: A Life of Lincoln*. New York: Viking Press, 1974.

Oates, Stephen B. *Abraham Lincoln: The Man Behind the Myths*. New York: NAL, 1984.

Obama, Barack. *The Audacity of Hope: Thoughts on Reclaiming the American Dream*. New York: Three Rivers Press, 2006.

Obama, Barack. *Dreams from My Father: A Story of Race and Inheritance*. New York: Three Rivers Press, 2004.

O'Brien, Cormac. *Secret Lives of U.S. Presidents: What Your Teachers Never Told You About the Men of the White House.* Philadelphia, PA: Quirk Books, 2004.

Prochnow, Herbert Victor. *Great Stories from Great Lives.* New York: Harper & Brothers, 1944.

Shenk, Joshua Wolf. *Lincoln's Melancholy: How Depression Challenged a President and Fueled His Greatness.* Boston: Houghton-Mifflin Company, 2005.

Smithsonian Books, Eds. *Every Four Years: The American Presidency, Revised Edition.* New York: W.W. Norton, 1984.

Wilson, Edmund. *Patriotic Gore: Studies in the Literature of the American Civil War.* New York: Oxford University Press, 1962.

Internet Sources

The American Presidency: A Glorious Burden. http://americanhistory.si.edu/presidency/home.html

The Avalon Project: The Inaugural Addresses of the Presidents
http://avalon.law.yale.edu/subject_menus/inaug.asp

Gettysburg National Military Park
http://www.pueblo.gsa.gov/cic_text/misc/gettysburg/index.htm

"I Do Solemnly Swear": Presidential Inaugurations
http://memory.loc.gov/ammem/pihtml/

The Joint Congressional Committee on Inaugural Ceremonies
http://inaugural.senate.gov/

The White House Historical Association
http://www.whitehousehistory.org/02/subs/02_b.html

Presidents of the United States
http://www.whitehouse.gov/history/presidents/